HUMAN MIND

HUMAN MIND

The space where it all begins

MANUEL TRIGUERO

First edition: May 2023
Title: HUMAN MIND
Cover image: Chicago
Copyright © 2023 Manuel Triguero
ISBN: 9798393443160

All rights reserved. It is strictly forbidden, without the written authorization of the copyright holders, under the sanctions established by law, the partial or total reproduction of this work by any means or process, including reprography and computer processing.

Hell is within you, as well as paradise. The truth is not found on the outside. No teacher, no writing can give it to you. It is within you and if you want to get it, look for it in your own company.

Osho

Index

Introduction *9*

1. Mental system 11
2. Confusion 62
3. Observation 94
4. Awareness 135
5. Control 158

Introduction

He who thinks that within himself he has no power and that in reality everything depends on the circumstances of life, will never be able to get to know that other dimension, that other world within us. One can rise above many negative circumstances of life if he knows his true "inner power", which is only acquired through the knowledge of ourselves.

You can only make your life beautiful if everything is born from your "inner power" and you do not let yourself be carried away and conditioned by the circumstances, by the context or by the conditioning of your own mind. It is another way of being in the world.

You are not born under a star that conditions you all your life, that forces you to be a certain way. In reality, the influences that you encounter throughout your life can be positive and negative, but they don't have to influence you in such a way that they end up leading you down a certain path. You must be above all that; find your "inner power" to build your own life, knowing how to overcome suffering: being above all those difficulties and problems that you encounter.

There is no being up there guiding you, leading you capriciously to a certain place and marking your destiny. It is you who with your actions are carving your own life and it is your mind and your wisdom that make you overcome difficulties and be above suffering.

When you learn to act of your own free will, then the future depends on you, not on circumstances or external influences; the future is always in your hands. If you do not understand this, your life will be a disaster, because you will think that everything depends on the context or circumstances, or on the external conditions that exist around you at any given moment.

In many occasions our own thoughts and actions are the ones that create problems and difficulties. That is why we must learn to rise above all that conditions us.

You reap what you sow; you are the fruit of your works. The destiny is actually created by oneself and should be related to what is the purpose of our life. Our destiny is what we should take care of, it is our most precious asset.

We must cultivate a destiny that takes us further and further away from suffering and makes us live in the present, where we must learn to overcome problems, to be above difficulties. We have the privilege of being able to choose our destiny, without the need to be tied to the conditioning of our own mind, of our human mind.

1. Mental System

January 1, 2020

Everything first appears in our mind and then influences us in other aspects of life. Everything is first written in the mind and is established there, where the origin of what we are, of what we end up doing, is found.

If we allow certain thoughts to dominate us, they will take shape on the outside; they will influence the way we behave, our relationships; they will be reproduced in our language, when we express ourselves: our words will be the prolongation of those thoughts that concur at that moment in our mind. If we come to understand this, we will understand many lived situations, we will understand the causes of that which causes us anguish, sadness, pain, emotional conflicts.

Everything dwells there first, it absorbs us through the thoughts that we hold when we pay attention to certain contents. Each thought is a piece of the mental puzzle that we all have inside. It drives us to perform actions, behaviors to which we become accustomed through the formation of habits.

Although we see certain behaviors as irrational, in the end we decide to keep repeating them simply because for us it is like an outlet to give free rein, to liberate those thoughts that, after so much repetition in that space, end up pressuring us.

Everything we do is first transmitted in our mind, it is the fruit of what we think; it is first formed in our consciousness, it inhabits and influences the quality of our actions: of what we do every day. Everything that belongs to our mind conditions the path we travel.

We embark on a current that is very difficult to stop, in such a way that it does not diminish with time, but can be maintained and even increase in strength. Everything that takes place there marks us in some way. All these processes remain and are repeated with the passage of time, they always accompany us and it seems that they never dissolve; we get used to them instead of trying to diminish them.

What is produced in our mind is the beginning of everything. Each thought is like a piece that tries to join with another, in such a way that it creates representations, structures that make us understand reality in a certain way during a period of time. It is like an automatic device that we all have, which has a great dimension and is part of our own nature.

January 2, 2020

Everything is first composed in our mind, that is why everything that happens in that space is important. We must be aware that some thoughts determine us, they are like a weed that grows until in the end it occupies everything and we cannot see anything clearly.

Our circumstances in life are the consequence of

everything that takes place there. Everything we do belongs first to our thoughts, which are published in our consciousness and gain intensity as we pay attention to them. Then, subsequently, they have an effect on us through our actions.

If we observe ourselves we will realize that this is so, that everything first has its center in our mind and from there we depend on how those components are organized, on the tendency they have. We will also realize that it is difficult to manage them, since their activity is very fast and their movement is practically automatic, it hardly gives us time to analyze what is happening there, to reduce the intensity when we are interested.

Everything has its root and origin in that space. It is there where everything is composed, through the contents that are introduced from our memory. It is not that there is a certain order, it is simply a mechanism that limits itself to transmit elements already stored until a set of similar thoughts is organized and from there a direction is established that is imposed on us. This direction is the one that in reality is marking us the way to follow, the actions that we must carry out in each moment and according to the circumstances.

This system is always accompanying us, in everything we do, in every reflection we have about any matter; it is a system that feeds itself.

January 3, 2020

Everything that is formed in our mind connects us with contents of the past that are in our memory. It is information that in some way we already possess because it has to do with our past experiences. They are contents that are stored in our memory and are not very new to us. In our mind they cross each other and create ideas, reasoning and points of view that influence us when we make our own decisions.

In practice, our mind works in this way. It is like a machine that is always on, that is part of our nature and that we must know it if we truly wish to change the direction of our own thoughts.

If we reflect a little we will understand many behaviors that we have had before. We will understand that everything that we are, in reality, has been previously fabricated there; that in the first place we have constructed everything before in our own consciousness.

When we name something from the outside, some object or whatever we want to point out at a given moment, it first appears in our mind, which has been busy looking for the name with which we have just qualified that object. When we already have the name then other related contents are added that help us to deepen the meaning of that object that we observe. If we realize that everything is first formed in our mind from the impressions we observe outside, in the context that surrounds us.

The most important information is produced first in that space, thanks to the ability of this mechanism to quickly search for related contents found in our memory. In this way we get to know what we see, what we have in front of us. Our mind is the one that facilitates all these operations that provide us with the necessary knowledge to be able to move through the world, to know what each thing is and to carry out the most appropriate actions according to each situation.

Everything is produced there first, thanks to all that information that our mind provides us with through a set of thoughts that are manufactured in it and that manifest themselves in our consciousness little by little.

January 4, 2020

Inside me I create a reality that often does not correspond to the one that exists outside. I also create the future inside me, in my own mind, through affirmations that I compose in which I try to anticipate what will happen to me later on.

All this is formed in the mind. Each manifestation that is established there has a meaning and a consequence. You will observe reality according to the contents that you have there at each moment, and what you think will happen in the future will also depend on the elements that at that moment govern and extend there, in that space.

Also each and every decision you make depends on the thoughts that are in your mind at any given moment and that you use to understand what is happening.

When you speak, each word you use is the consequence of a thought that at that moment is going through your mind and that you cannot prevent, you cannot hide. You feel the need to express it through language, through words. The same happens with each of your behaviors: they are the consequence of an accumulation of thoughts that form a structure so strong that finally they are transformed into action. This thought structure composes what you should do at any given moment, depending on the situation you are in.

Our internal dialogue, during all the time, is nothing more than the consequence of all those thoughts that manifest themselves over and over again in that space. We simply repeat those terms that appear in our consciousness and that develop as we pay attention to them. They are distributed throughout our mind as objects, as thoughts that are produced one after another, while we have the feeling that we can do nothing to avoid them, to free ourselves from them and stop this system that does not stop and that seems to have no end.

All this that takes place first in our mind is shaping who we are, our personality, everything we think and what we do throughout the day. It also influences our own relationships, when we establish contact with those people who surround us in the context in which we live. Our way of relating is also influenced by what happens in our mind at every moment, because it dictates to us what we should say, how we should act before those around us.

What is produced in our mind is what forces us to act in a certain way, depending on the situation. Sometimes we can even have contradictory behaviors: that can be the origin of the order to behave in a certain way in one situation and to act in the opposite way in another different situation. The mind adapts to the different contexts in which our life develops.

That is why we often have so many contradictions, both in our own behavior and in our way of thinking. We try to adapt ourselves to each situation, to the characteristics of the people we relate to. Depending on how those people are, we can have one attitude or another; it is a form of survival.

Our mind is the one that guides us, that directs us, and with each option it extracts consequences and a reading that it then uses to establish the following actions and what we should think about later, in a similar situation.

All this is done automatically by our mind, without our being aware of it. It is a hidden activity that has no end, that does not decline, that is always there, introducing thoughts, ideas, images in our consciousness, in such a way that our attention is always located there, in what happens in that space where everything starts, where our way of thinking is organized, our way of seeing the world and everything that happens around us.

January 5, 2020

Depending on the size of the activity of our own thoughts and the effort with which we pay attention to those contents, they will acquire strength in our mind and we will not forget them so easily, they will find a cavity in our consciousness and will draw a reality that will be consolidated over time.

If we examine attentively what goes through our mind we will realize that everything that affects us is there. Everything that is of interest to us first arises there.

Also all our contradictions and our emotional conflicts are taking shape, are acquiring a presence within that space. We only need to examine ourselves a little to really realize that this mental movement, which is constantly taking place within us and which is very difficult for us to understand, slowly surrounds us and shapes what we are and what we do.

Everything arises first in the territory of our mind. Everything is first composed there, even the words we express with our language first maintain a form in our consciousness; everything is produced there first.

The starting point is always our mind and everything that is projected and constructed there. There lies the most important part of our conflicts, of our difficulties. Everything depends on the way in which a series of contents in the form of thoughts come together; that in reality is what sets everything else in motion, everything that follows, which in most cases we do not manage to stop, in such a way that we accommodate ourselves to this way of functioning of this system, although the consequences are not good for us in the long term and we find many contradictions within us that then manifest themselves on the outside, in our way of acting, in our attitudes.

If we light our inner lamp we will realize this. We just need to get used to seeing it; with a little willpower on our part we can achieve it.

January 6, 2020

We function this way by nature, it is the mechanism in us that makes it possible for there to be an inner communication, a whole inner world in the deepest part of ourselves.

The words, our language, everything starts from there. It is in our consciousness where we group our thoughts, where we give order to our words, to what we are going to say.

It is there where we interpret the events we observe outside, where our reflections and reasoning take place when we try to look for an explanation to a concrete situation we have before us.

It is where all those contents stored in our memory arise that make us have emotions, which are transmitted throughout our body and many of them are clearly visible on the outside.

It is where our beliefs and our ideas are produced, our points of view, which in many occasions can become contradictory because there is so much information that we handle that we hardly have time to establish an order and achieve a certain coherence in our arguments and expositions.

Everything manifests itself there first, what we are going to do or what we decide not to do because at that moment we do not consider it useful. It is the place where the decisions that will later mark our destiny, our way of life, are first made. Our current state is also due to that space where each of the behaviors and habits that have led us to be what we are at every moment have been woven.

That is why it is important that we fix our gaze on that space where everything starts, which is our mind, especially to see if we can do something to intervene on it, to not let ourselves be manipulated by certain processes that occur there and of which we barely have control.

It is important because it is a mechanism that determines what we end up being, that influences us in everything we end up doing throughout the day. Because what we do consciously is not the same as what we do in a mechanical, automatic way, as if we had been programmed to do exactly that.

For all these reasons, this space where our decisions take place is relevant, as well as most of the conflicts and problems that we create for ourselves because we do not have enough ability to find the solutions in those moments when we need them.

January 7, 2020

In reality, that which causes us sadness or suffering or influences our own will, begins and depends on that mechanism that determines us without us being conscious of it many times.

All our emotional wounds have been created there, through a series of determined thoughts that have made us have a specific vision about something that has happened to us.

If we go a little deeper inside ourselves, we will also understand that our personality, our character depends, is a function of everything that is articulated in our mind. Everything begins there first, in our consciousness, and then moves out of us.

Our personality is the result of the functioning of our own mind; it is the direct result of what we think in each moment. We build everything from there. Our personality is a framework that we build according to our most habitual thoughts, which are composed and united with other similar ones without us having too much control.

It is the source of our personality, which is then reflected on the outside, in our behavior, in our attitudes and in our way of expressing ourselves and being with others. Our personality is also forged in that space, where all those processes that make us behave in a certain way take place.

Everything that is emitted in our mind, also forms part of our personality, because we function based on that, based on that repetitive mechanism that all living beings have, which is a system by which a series of thoughts try to develop over others, depending on the attention, the importance that we give them.

In this way they determine our life, our language, our way of seeing the world, our way of acting; we basically depend on that. It is as if we were obliged to follow, without further ado, this mechanism that runs mechanically within us and that shows us the way to follow, step by step.

Our mind, in reality, is the seed of what we are, although this is so, we have the capacity to reach a certain mastery of this system. Everything is a function of the attention we pay to certain contents. Everything is a function of where we put our focus of attention.

January 8, 2020

We depend on this mechanism that we execute automatically without realizing it, while in our mind one thought after another is added in a sequence, through an order that has no end. We compose our own mental movies that sometimes are related to what is really happening, but sometimes are not: at other times they are quite distant from reality and the time in which we live.

All this is formed in our mind and shapes our way of understanding the world, our way of seeing life. When something causes us a daze, confuses us, it first arises there, in such a way that it may not be easily extinguished, since it is due to a kind of thoughts that are never interrupted, that do not hide, that appear in that place that is our consciousness, in such a way that they are joining with other similar thoughts and are trapping us and influencing our state of mind, they are indicating us the step we should take at every moment.

They are elements that take hold of us, that prepare us to act. They attract our attention because their content, for some reason, is significant and that is why they establish themselves in our consciousness, and that is what causes them to keep arising until they form a set of thoughts that manifest themselves in such a way that in the end they end up influencing us: they have an effect on us, they indicate us what kind of actions we should carry out and the moment in which we have to do them; we cannot separate ourselves from them so easily, because they have a place in our consciousness and become part of our internal conversation, of our inner dialogue.

January 9, 2020

We do not train the ability to focus on our mind, on what we are thinking about. Our mental functioning is like a program that runs by itself, automatically, without us intervening in a conscious way on it.

That is why we must be careful with what happens there, with what we think, with the contents we handle and pay attention to, because that is the starting point for our actions, our opinions and our way of understanding the world and everything around us. The quality of our own life depends on the quality of our thoughts, that is why our mental functioning and everything that happens in the space of our own consciousness is so important.

If we concentrate on our thoughts we can observe the direction they want to take, we can glimpse those that are most repeated and those that are decreasing, those that are becoming smaller and smaller in our consciousness. It is a movement that seems to have no end, it is like an inexhaustible activity that always tries to propose things to us, that can even distort reality when a series of determined thoughts come together and cause us to have a wrong vision of things.

We must be careful with everything that is expressed in our mind, because it influences our way of understanding the world, of understanding life and the people around us. Everything that manifests itself in that space has a great influence, a great power over us. Our interpretation of everything that happens to us depends on the contents that we have in our mind at each moment, on the elements that are circulating at that moment in our consciousness.

It is necessary that we know this, that we take it very much into account, because everything that develops in our mind can then manifest itself outside, in everything we do, in what we say when there is someone around us. Everything has its origin there first, in that mechanism that has the power to guide us in a certain direction, in the direction that in each moment dictate the thoughts that are at that moment in our consciousness.

January 11, 2020

Our mental system is like this: it is very repetitive. Almost always the same thoughts occupy the same spaces in an automatic way. Our mind is constantly retrieving content from our memory. It is like a repetitive process that is downloading previous information and all this is producing an effect on us, which causes a series of emotional responses, behavior, a series of reactions on our part, to all those contents that this mechanism is presenting us and to which we end up adapting. Everything that is represented in our mind, therefore, is part of a process that has an effect on us.

Depending on the quantity and quality of information in our mind at any given moment, we will act in one way or another. It depends on the intensity of those thoughts and the importance we give them. In that same measure they will be expanded in our conscience and will originate behaviors and answers before the stimuli that exist outside.

When something awakens our interest, we try to look for an explanation, we try to discover something more about that subject. We ask ourselves questions when we face situations that we do not understand, that we do not control. We try to look for answers within ourselves, we try to investigate a little bit about some of our past experiences, to get some information to help us understand what we do not know at first. We are always trying to control every situation that comes our way. It is as if we have the need to always seek security in everything we do, in everything we think, so that the results of our actions are always in line with what we expect to happen.

Sometimes we reflect to try to guess the causes of some things that happen to us, to try to learn from them, to know how many things that we do not know work, to know the reasons.

Some important events in our life, in some way, condition us. We identify ourselves with everything we think, with everything we observe around us. Somehow we adapt them to our judgments, to our thoughts, which then will condition us, because they will provide us with a way of understanding life that will guide us in a certain direction.

In many occasions our thought processes are not rational, although we try to make them so. In many occasions we let ourselves be guided by interested judgments and far from the truth: from what really happens. All this develops in us a way of understanding the world that is a little far from reality.

Let's say that we create in us an interested vision of life, of what happens. It depends on the point of view that we have in each moment and the type of thoughts that we use to associate things with others. All this conditions our way of seeing reality, in such a way that in the end we may give relevance to things that have no relevance and that in the end we do not learn anything from important experiences that happen to us.

It depends on the type of movement and the orientation of our own thoughts. Therefore, our way of evaluating everything that happens to us influences and conditions us in a considered way.

The way we associate our judgments, our ideas, can bring us closer to or move us away from reality. The type of connection that we establish between each of our thoughts, will build a model, a way of seeing the world, the life that surrounds us.

Our way of interpreting the results of our own experiences also influences us. The explanations we find about all those things that happen around us will also influence the type of responses we give with our behaviors.

In fact, everything that goes on in our mind, intervenes in our way of interpreting reality. The impact of the things that happen to us also influences the type of reflections we make.

January 12, 2020

We are always involved in a large number of thoughts that are scattered through our mind. When there is a shortage of contents, our mind is in charge of rescuing them from our memory, in such a way that it constantly feeds itself with elements that we have already stored as a result of our previous experiences.

Our mind uses the contents we have stored in our memory to feed its constant and repetitive movement. It never stops because there is a large amount of information that we have accumulated throughout our lives and there will always be elements to occupy our mind in some way.

In our internal dialogue, in that inner conversation that we often have with ourselves, we can observe it clearly. They are only thoughts that we verbalize internally and that have to do with some recent event that manages to occupy our attention. At that moment many reflections come to us that we say to ourselves, but if we look at all of them we make them based on a mental movement that allows us to relate some thoughts with others, some contents that we already have with others, in such a way that in the end we draw a series of conclusions that help us to orient ourselves through life, to make decisions; although many of them are not the most accurate and then we realize it with time.

All mental objects are elements that we already have stored, that we have been acquiring through our past experiences. They have been introduced into our memory. Some are more recent and others are more distant, but any of them can arise at any time in that space, become a mental representation that can give rise to a thought, an idea, an image that once it enters our mind can influence in such a way that it can capture our attention, keep us there for a certain time.

They are contents stored in the past that, if they become very repetitive, can influence us in such a way that they cause us to act in a certain direction, in a direction related to those contents. It all depends on how much attention we pay to them, how long we are attentive to that information, that thought or that idea.

This is how our mind works. It has a great influence on us because it is the one that at a given moment can determine the direction in which we should move. It is leading the way in some way. Therefore, everything that is expressed in that space is of great importance, because it provides us with the way to move through life, to be in the world and to relate to the people around us.

January 14, 2020

Circumstances often incline us to act in a certain

way, they predispose us to go in a certain direction, and we are not aware that in most cases these circumstances are the consequence of our own previous actions, they are the effect of what we have previously built in our mind.

When we become aware that this is so we have an instrument in our hands to direct our actions, since these enclose all those thoughts that impulsively then accumulate in that space, many times without our consent.

Everything we do on the outside belongs to the world of our consciousness, everything we speak first acquires a form there; then we throw it outside in the form of words, when we use our language or through our actions, our attitudes.

The world we build is a function of everything that rests in our consciousness. If there is any alteration in it, because at that moment the movement of thoughts is contradictory, this will take shape outside of us: in our way of expressing ourselves, in our relationships, in our way of observing everything that happens around us.

When a series of thoughts take over our consciousness, they try to find a way out of us. If there is conflict within us, we transfer it to our relationships, to our way of acting; it will be seen in our attitude.

Everything we think has an effect inside and outside of us. Everything is diffused outside in one way or another, depending on the direction taken by those contents that accumulate in our mind, coming from our memory.

January 15, 2020

Our mind is a territory that still remains to be explored, it is a place where there is always a large volume of information, often opposing, which creates conflicts that establish a distance with reality, with what is really happening outside. It is information that creates subjective sensations about those things that happen to us every day. It leads us to draw conclusions that have no relation with reality, and all this can influence us in our well-being, in our way of facing the difficulties we encounter every day.

We are the ones who feed this mechanism, the ones who cause similar thoughts to temporarily accumulate, and this is due to the focus of our attention. This is what causes certain contents to expand in our mind and not others.

These thoughts arise, appear in our consciousness, on the screen that is our consciousness; they show themselves there. They have an intention: they invite us to continue reflecting on them, or to a specific action related to those thoughts.

They can influence our emotions. They also join with other similar thoughts and establish themselves there, in our intellect, creating a link with our consciousness that is difficult for us to eliminate.

January 16, 2020

To classify all the information stored in our memory would be an impossible task. We can only observe some contents that are collected in our consciousness; in these cases we can qualify these contents as positive or negative, see the possible influence they can exert on us.

In a narrow margin of time a great amount of information moves through our mind, and therefore it is difficult to order it, to discard that which is not useful. Later, when we perform some action as a consequence of this previous information that appears in our mind, we can evaluate if those thoughts are constructive or not for us.

Therefore, depending on our situation, we can draw conclusions about the type of content that exists at any given moment in that space. If our path is the right one, then we will conclude that our thoughts are going in the right direction; if, on the contrary, we do not feel fulfilled with what we are doing, we can intuit that perhaps we are making a mistake in something, possibly in our way of thinking or planning our own actions.

Everything that moves in our intellect then has a consequence, in one way or another, on the outside, in our daily life. Depending on how we feed our mind, our actions will go in one direction or another; this will be reflected in our behaviors, which in the end will create our circumstances and the situation in which we live in each moment.

January 17, 2020

Our whole life is a continuous learning process. All the information we accumulate helps us to understand what is happening. Subsequently, thanks to the accumulated experiences, we can understand the reality that surrounds us and adapt, in this way, our behaviors to the context in which we live.

It also helps us to understand behaviors, our own and those of all the people around us. To become aware of many factors, both external and internal, that exist in reality and that influence us. Thanks to the accumulated learning we can find explanations to everything that happens to us.

We only have to reflect, objectively, and we will immediately find the causes of what happens to us. It is a matter of investigating a little, of being observers. Then we will see how our mind produces a series of conclusions about life and the world in which we live. Contents related to the knowledge of ourselves will appear, so that at the end we will have an approximate idea of what we are.

All the information that comes to us from outside, fills our reason with concepts that help us to understand the world, because they give us an answer about many things that we do not know or that we do not understand.

Thanks to the accumulated information we can understand the events that happen, the different characteristics of reality; have a personal approach to anything that happens.

All our previous experiences give us the possibility to develop a series of skills necessary to develop in the context where we live, to adapt to all the changes that occur.

Those who acquire more experiences have more advantages over others who have accumulated less information about the environment in which they live.

If we understand the principles and mechanisms that govern our internal life, we will understand our psychological functioning and our behaviors, our way of reacting to the events that happen to us.

What we observe outside, all that accumulated information, will help us to respond appropriately to the demands of our environment. We will know how to choose the most convenient behaviors to solve the difficulties that arise throughout our life.

Everything depends on the information with which we feed our brain; on the reading we make of each and every one of the experiences we have. Our answers, our way of facing life, will depend on all of this.

Our internal system, our mental structure, will be built according to this. Our understanding will be directed towards one place or another depending on the information we have, depending on the contents that exist in our memory, the result of past experiences. All these elements will be presented in our mind, forming a structure, a response system.

Our way of thinking, in some way, is the result of all that information accumulated over the years. It is an information that will be grouped in our memory and that will be presented little by little in our consciousness, as we need it.

We only need to pay attention to be sensitive, to be aware of all that is produced in our intellect, because that is where the answers are born and also the impediments that we find when we face a problematic situation.

In that space is where the whole process that leads to what ends up being our circumstances begins. That is why everything that takes place in that place is important. All the processes that take place there have an effect on our life, on our way of reacting to problems or to the stimuli that exist outside; everything depends on our mental mechanism.

Also our emotional response, our way of relating, the way we use our affectivity, our habits. Everything has a previous representation in that space.

If it is repetitive, in the end it ends up leading us, conditioning us, in some way. A system is created within us that in the end ends up directing our behaviors, and when we get used to it, it is difficult to modify it.

If you carefully observe your behaviors, you will realize, you will discover, that there is a whole process behind that leads you to respond in a certain way when you are faced with a series of stimuli. It is we ourselves who condition ourselves, who allow our mind to show us the way.

January 18, 2020

Everything is a product of the mind. Everything is the result of the contents that are first gathered in that space. Depending on the way we deal with those contents, then the final product will emerge, which will be for us like an information by which we will be guided. That information will be the one that will establish the direction we should take.

Sometimes it is a disordered information, which leads us in many occasions to confusion, because we do not manage to establish an order in all those thoughts that crowd in the mind, that live in it for long periods of time if we give them importance.

If we understand that those thoughts are principal for us or particular for some reason, they can remain there for a long time, feeding our reason. They will have a tendency to repeat themselves constantly, attributing meanings to everything we observe. They are thoughts that will progress over time within us, they will become larger and larger depending on the time they are occupying our consciousness.

There are thoughts of great size that we cannot hide easily, that it is difficult for them to dissolve with time, since they refer to very significant experiences for us, in such a way that they influence our sadness or our happiness, depending on whether they have been positive or negative experiences.

Everything that exists in our intellect provides us with a path, a vision of the world, it forms in us a reality that we can find outside or not. We depend in some way on everything that is built inside us, on everything that is in our consciousness at any given moment, on everything that settles in our mind, that shows itself in the form of thoughts, images and mental objects.

All these contents never seem to end, since they are repeated over and over again throughout the length and breadth of our consciousness. This is the origin of our desires, our illusions, our projects, when one idea is united with another, in such a way that they sow a future with which we feel identified.

They are thoughts that transmit knowledge to us, in such a way that we learn from each content that arises in that space, when it is united with other similar contents.

Our mind creates, therefore, the knowledge of things. We acquire new information as these contents are organized with each other. As they come together, they give shape to a way of seeing things, they generate new reflections and make us reach new conclusions about what is happening to us at each moment.

January 19, 2020

One of the main characteristics of our mind is that it relates some contents with others, in such a way that finally it elaborates a set of thoughts, reflections and conclusions that later become important for us, since these new contents somehow guide us. They are what we use to interpret what is happening around us: all those things that surround us.

We draw conclusions based on the way we have previously related our thoughts from past experiences. Everything in our mind seems to be linked by a thread that it itself creates according to the elements that are important to us, or according to the thoughts to which we pay most attention.

All these contents wait there, in our memory, waiting to come out and grow in our consciousness. They are expressed one after the other, they accumulate in our understanding as water accumulates on the ground, and from there we tolerate, we allow that water to start flowing without knowing where it will arrive, what will happen to us.

The fact is that all those elements of our memory are dissolving in that place; some even take root in it, depending on the importance they have for us and the attention we pay to them; it is like a process that never ends.

But it is important to understand this procedure; to be aware that we function in this way. This leads us to consider that if at some point in our lives there is something that worries us, that causes us suffering, it is exactly due to this process by which a series of thoughts -in this case negative- are established in our mind, which are joined with other similar ones, in such a way that in the end they lead us to draw a series of certain conclusions, to have a series of reflections about ourselves that indicate to us the course we should follow in some way.

Without knowing it, we are subject to this process, to this procedure that our own reason follows and that creates a universe, a concrete atmosphere in our conscience that makes us see reality in a certain way.

These kinds of thoughts, as they are repeated, take on a form, they are refined, so to speak, they increase their influence on us. There are thoughts that can bring us happiness and others can lead us to restlessness and suffering, but everything starts from that place; it is there where the changes of our state of mind take place; it is there where the origin of our emotions, of our feelings is. It all depends on the tendency of the thoughts that we have in that space at any given moment.

January 21, 2020

Your thoughts are chained in your mind in a fast way. If you are not aware of it, you remain ignorant of this process, which accelerates without you noticing it, in such a way that new contents are added, one after the other, so that they are constantly rushing through your intellect and rising in your consciousness.

Some thoughts are increasing, especially when they are chained with other similar ones, creating new structures that make you inclined to think in a certain way, due to all those thoughts that are accumulating with each other. In the end you develop a series of ideas that occupy a large space in your mind and that in the end submerge you in a certain way of understanding the world.

There are many thoughts that lodge there, for long periods of time, and are not suppressed: they have a series of characteristics that make them difficult to eliminate.

Thoughts that are similar join with each other and anticipate others that are weaker, that are less frequent. All those thoughts that are to your liking, increase, expand in some way in your consciousness, which is the showcase, so to speak, of all that content that is in your memory.

All those representations that you have been keeping over the years, the fruit of your past experiences, gradually emerge there and are strengthened to the extent that you attach importance to them.

When you concentrate on a series of concrete thoughts, they increase, the number of representations related to that content grows and is affirmed as you pay attention to it.

Sometimes they become so strong that it is difficult to free yourself from them. It is as if they accelerate and you cannot control them. To achieve a certain moderation over them, it is necessary to be aware of all that is in that extension that is your consciousness.

To do this you must recognize, observe those contents that try to appropriate your attention, that incline you to act in a certain way. It is a question of protecting yourself a little, since the usual thing is to become accustomed to a form of thought, to follow the current of all those mental images that extend in your conscience without rest, that go filling of arguments, of subjects, all your reason, through the association of similar contents, that when they join it is difficult to separate, since they become stronger, causing in this way the repetition of the same thoughts.

It is possible to recognize and examine these processes if you manage to pause through silence. Then you become aware of all that is hidden within you, in your inner world. They are hidden processes, but they incite you to think in a specific way and in many cases they sow confusion in you, when they are negative contents that pierce you inside and separate you from what you really are, from your essence.

January 22, 2020

When it comes to very intense thoughts, we can hardly do anything to stop that mental movement. When the materials that our mind uses are very significant for us, such as memories of the past that marked us, they manage to have a great influence, so that they make us feel high emotions. This kind of thoughts is difficult to stop, since they are associated with past experiences that were very important to us, that determined us in some way.

On the other hand, when it comes to irrelevant thoughts, they do not develop so strongly, they seem to be more flexible and less consistent, so that they are easily diluted and lose their presence in our consciousness. In this last case this kind of contents do not influence us so much, because they are relative thoughts or of little importance for us.

There are also useless thoughts that try to express themselves in this space. Sometimes we do give them importance, although in reality they are worthless, because they do not lead to anything. They simply manifest themselves and are repeated over and over again until they manage to capture all our attention; they even make it possible for us to carry out some action related to them, but in reality they are of no visible use to us: they are thoughts and actions that lead nowhere, they only make us waste our valuable time and energy.

In this last case we must be attentive when we see ourselves performing some action or behavior in which we clearly see that we are wasting our time. This is not difficult to detect, simply by observing ourselves we will realize it instantly.

As we see, everything that occurs in our mind is setting the pattern to follow, so it has a great influence on us. Knowing this is the first step to understand ourselves, to find explanations for everything we do and what we have done before. All this is what explains our situation at every moment of our life; all this is what is behind our own circumstances.

If we watch our own behavior we will know at once that behind it there is a mental movement composed of thoughts that have formed in our consciousness and have had that effect upon us. Out of all the abundance of thoughts there may be at that moment, our consciousness has chosen a class of thoughts that has caused us to take a particular action.

January 23, 2020

Everything exists first in our mind; we constantly create things through it. We can create fear, which will end up frightening us, and we can also create joy, depending on the moment we are in, on the present situation.

Everything is first articulated there. It is like a constant movie that never ends and that provides us with our lifestyle; it shapes our moods, our attitudes, even our own actions.

Everything is first constituted and composed within our own intellect, and it does it in an automatic way, many times without us noticing it, so it is a mechanism that has hardly any regulation.

When we are overwhelmed by many thoughts at the same time, we are somehow unable to reduce them. In that instant we do not have a procedure through which we can extinguish all those thoughts that are multiplying, that are increasing. In most cases we are subject to this mechanism, without being able to count on an instrument to be able to control it.

We can notice the thoughts that are taking place at any given moment; the images that are represented there; we can become aware of the abundance of ideas on a given subject at a given moment; we can become aware of the diversity of thoughts that we have, of how they remain there for a long time, if we finally pay attention to them.

We can also become aware of how they unite with other similar ones; of how, on some occasions, we suffer a mental shock, a conflict, when we observe that we have contradictory thoughts in a short space of time that in no way benefit us, because this ends up sowing doubts and makes the information we have and our knowledge invalid to solve the difficulty or the problem we are trying to solve at that moment.

Many times this kind of mental conflicts extend over time, until a moment comes when we manage to separate those thoughts that cause us conflict and that are not useful for us.

In this sense, thoughts are like objects, forms that we can move, that we can reduce, but if we are aware of them: if we pay attention to these processes that develop in our mind, which are the cause of our behavior on the outside; they are the ones that mark our way of relating to others; they are the beginning of everything.

January 25, 2020

If we make an interval, we will realize the amount of mental programs that are registered in our mind, which have been established there because we have repeated in a mechanical way the same thoughts, with the same frequency, so that in the end a series of contents have been imposed that make up these programs that become constant. If we repeat them frequently, they are distributed throughout that space, at the same time that we are reinforcing them without realizing it.

These same programs are the ones that provide us with the answers we should give, the type of thoughts we should have, the way in which they should be distributed throughout our consciousness.

They manage to function autonomously, they do not depend on what we decide, because in the end they are executed in a mechanical way and are reinforced even more if at the end we perform a series of behaviors that have to do with the contents of these programs.

Once they are installed in our mind, it is difficult to control them; it is difficult to extinguish them. To do so, we will have to go to the beginning, to analyze a little the thoughts that provoked them.

In this way, we will come to understand how they have developed; the way they are executed; how the different contents are presented and what we experience when all those elements arise there; then we will know better their characteristics and we will be able to identify the elements of which they are composed. We will realize how we feed them ourselves.

These mental programs then have a great effect on us; once they are set in motion, there seems to be no end to them.

Many of our habits, our habitual behaviors, are the fruit of these programs, which we ourselves build up over time, reinforcing them through our own mechanical and repetitive behaviors.

Once we know their characteristics and are aware that they exist, we can try to change them if they are not beneficial for us. To do this we need a certain amount of time. It is not so easy to change our mental activity, to convert it into a different one, to try to find other alternatives that are healthier for us.

All these mental programs have been built through time and it will be through time that we will be able to correct them. It is not that we have to follow a specific procedure, it is only that we pay attention to our own behaviors, since our behaviors are the result of all those thoughts and programs that we have installed in our mind.

If we make an effort to correct some of our behaviors, many of those mental programs will begin to decrease their activity, they will not be reinforced, since the system of behaviors will be different. This is what may determine that we have results in terms of eliminating some of the mental programs that take place in that space.

January 26, 2020

Understanding the language of the mind is possible. We can get to the root of what we think if we connect with that inner space where similar thoughts are simultaneously arising. If we are aware of those elements that are taking shape in our consciousness, we will find the meaning of our actions, of all those things we do every day, of our behaviors, of our way of understanding the world, since all that is composed there, in that place.

We only try to imitate what we have on the screen of our consciousness. Our own emotions first originate there, in the form of thoughts, and then have an effect on our organism. Our intentions also start from there, from that mental movement which has an effect on us and which is carried out through a whole series of thoughts coming from our memory.

All the contents that appear in our mind are conjugated with each other, they occupy a certain place in that mental space. Some are repeated more frequently than others, until they form a block, a structure that is then difficult to stop. In this way, a certain way of thinking is built, through which we understand the reality of all those things that happen to us.

Thanks to this mental structure we are looking for the reasons, the causes of everything we experience. Thanks to this system we forge our destiny, which is nothing more than the result of the movement of our reason that is produced through our thoughts. All our reasoning, our conclusions and reflections also arise from there. Those that we repeat more frequently, those that are more important to us, because they are more useful to us or for any other reason, acquire a greater position.

January 27, 2020

Everything seems to come together in our mind. It is like a box where all the necessary tools to solve any situation, any conflict, are found. In it we can produce the solutions we need to solve a particular difficulty.

Although the information that we have stored there is very diverse and it seems that it is not very well organized, because when we need to clarify ourselves in some matter, many times we do not know which direction to take, and this is due to the effect of the amount of information that we have, which in many occasions can even be contradictory, because we can think one thing and the opposite at the same time.

Depending on the circumstances, depending on the situation we are going through, we can have a mental discourse in one sense or another. Our intellect is always working, causing us to constantly have to use words to express what is manifesting in each moment in our consciousness. We are always trying to find explanations for everything we do or feel.

All this is driven by the lines of thought that constantly appear there, as elements that shape a way of acting, a way of understanding the world. All this causes us to move in a certain direction, to become accustomed to a series of habits that we gradually secure over time, by dint of repeating them over and over again.

That is why our way of acting, our habits, are usually always the same. Our mind is like a spring where thoughts keep gushing out, which we name, to which we attribute a meaning according to the experiences we have had previously.

All these elements that appear in that space are intertwined with each other, are united with contents that are common and thus build a structure, a mental body that once it takes root, once it is established, it is very difficult to change; we cannot replace it so easily. This is how our way of understanding the world, of understanding reality, is composed over time.

Every time we try to give a meaning to everything that happens to us, we resort to this mental structure already established in our consciousness, and from there we begin to assemble our own movie; our own interpretation of reality, which sometimes may be wrong, may not be true.

Therefore, with time, we are surprised that what we find in reality does not correspond with what we had previously thought, with what we had mentally established. In these cases a division is created between reality and our own vision of things: our interpretation of the world.

When there is a great division, a great distance between these two aspects, we find real existential difficulties. When there is not so much distance or there is a similarity between reality and what we think, everything seems to go well, we do not have any problem.

January 29, 2020

In our mind many ideas are constantly expressed, as if it were a computer program in charge only of producing reflections, conclusions that are joined with each other until they create their own theories about the functioning of the world, of reality.

All this is done autonomously by our intellect, without us having to make any effort on our part. It is programmed to easily join some thoughts with others when they are related, as well as ideas and contents until they form a structure that has a foundation and a meaning.

Once a series of elements begin to unite and create a system of thought, our reason is already predisposed to function along the lines of that structure or system. Once it begins to function in this way, it is difficult to establish changes and separate the elements of that mental structure. When we get used to think in a certain way about certain issues, then it is quite complicated to change the chip, change our point of view and turn around our own thoughts.

This homogeneous way of thinking that we have in many occasions can lead us in some cases to a very strict way of seeing things, of understanding the world. In this way we pigeonhole our approaches and decisions and do not contemplate other alternatives. We are blinded by our own personal point of view and from there we act, without taking into account other possibilities, other options.

Many times we let ourselves be pigeonholed by our own intellect and this prevents us from discovering other alternatives that also exist, that we can also contemplate but that we do not do so because our mind blinds us and leads us only in a direction that it itself establishes according to the kind of contents that have been added and that have formed a whole structure of thought, a whole mental system that is what actually makes us function in a certain way.

With time and with the results of our own experience, we modify this structure, according to the reading that we make of the results obtained from our own experience. From there we eliminate elements that no longer serve us or we see that they do not correspond to reality and we add new ones. In this way we are modifying our mental system, through the experiences that we are experiencing.

Our mind is a movement that never stops and is always in permanent change, although many of our reasonings keep repeating themselves over and over again. One of the main characteristics is repetition, but at the same time changes are also established in some thoughts that progressively begin to diminish to make way for new ones that try to open a gap in our consciousness.

Therefore, our mental structure is a system that changes over time, although these changes are slow and we have the feeling that it is always in the same place, that there is no movement. We can maintain the same ideas for long periods of time, but a circumstance may occur that modifies our own point of view in such a way that some ideas that remain unchanged within our mental system may disappear in place of others that take their place.

Much of our learning is produced by trial and error. What we think at any given time about a particular subject may change depending on the experiences we have the occasion to live in our daily lives.

January 30, 2020

Our mind is a constant mechanism that produces thoughts, images; it recovers contents from the past that are stored in our memory and that compose within us a certain reality, an internal discourse that we can clearly observe in our inner voice, in that dialogue that we often have with ourselves, where we try to understand what is happening to us at a given moment. They compose a way of seeing reality that conditions us, that gives meaning to all those things we do.

When we focus on this kind of thoughts, at the same time we are eliminating other thoughts, because in those moments we are focusing on those concrete objects, on those forms and not on others, which are also within our mental structure.

The key is to find a way to modulate this structure, to analyze its qualities, to see how it is being ordered. This capacity of analysis can be a good instrument to reach a certain control over it, because this mental structure is the one that in the end manufactures our way of thinking, our way of seeing the world.

If we have the tendency to see things in a certain way, it is because of this mental structure, which is nothing more than the set of thoughts that have been placed there, joining one with another, thanks to the movement that occurs in the mind constantly and automatically This mental structure is an arsenal of different contents that have some relationship, and that is why they are joining one with another over time.

February 1, 2020

What arises in our mind determines our destiny, so we must be attentive to the form of all those contents that arise and are constantly present in our consciousness. It is required that there is an order in all that group of elements, which play a very important role because they influence us in the rest of the things we do.

In our intellect, without realizing it, we are constructing a building that then has an effect on the external level. It is a building made up of thoughts, images, ideas, reflections, conclusions, which gradually settles over time and takes shape through a foundation that we ourselves are building without realizing it, by constantly repeating a series of thoughts that are usually always the same.

These thoughts have a series of qualities that call our attention and that is why they are repeated more frequently, because we give them more importance than others. In this way a building is constructed that forms our mentality; it is built with all these elements.

Some arise from our memory and others are produced in our consciousness, when we voluntarily join one thought with another. We plant small seeds that later take on a greater dimension, in such a way that new ideas, new currents of thought and other ways of understanding the world around us begin to sprout in that space.

The most repeated thoughts have the property that they are similar to each other, as if they belonged to the same family. They are the ones we use frequently in our internal dialogue, which are the ones that guide, in some way, our vision of things. They establish a certain mental order that influences us, because it is part of a mental structure that is built over time.

Our ideas, reasoning, belong to that determined mental structure that can vary with the passage of time. Our mentality, our way of seeing the world, is expressed in the words we use, in the language we use, in our attitudes, in our moods and in our emotions; they have an effect on us and anyone who is a little observant can detect it.

February 2, 2020

We unwittingly give shape to a series of ideas which in this way become secure in our minds. Then comes to us an abundance of thoughts related to these ideas, similar thoughts are collected and we are conducting ourselves in this way.

In our thought there is a series of ideas that are principal and others secondary; this is indicated by the meaning that we give to each one of them: depending on the importance that they have for us, we give them one form or another.

For our ideas to be formed, all these thoughts must have a direction: they must be in agreement with each other; they must belong to the same field of contents so that everything has a sense, a meaning.

All this is being composed in our mind. It is very difficult to stop this process that runs automatically and replaces some thoughts with others.

This is how this whole mechanism works. Sometimes it does it with a great intensity, when a great number of thoughts accumulates, and in other occasions it seems to be that our mind is less active, it depends on the tranquility that we have, if we know how to find the calm, somehow; although almost always there is a multitude of images in all that set of contents that appear in our conscience.

This way of functioning belongs to our own nature and we can hardly stop it. What we can do is to be aware that this is how it works, that there is a series of thoughts that are always accompanying us in that space and that they are nothing more than contents that belong to our memory.

When they unite with each other, they form ideas that determine us, that guide us in our way of acting. We, almost unintentionally, follow that current that starts there and that shapes our life, what we do, the way we relate to others.

In our mind are created the arguments we need to reason, to find a certain clarity in what happens to us. Through our reason we try to look for solutions to our own difficulties; sometimes we find them and sometimes we don't, it depends on the information we have in those moments in our consciousness.

Through this information we draw conclusions that guide us in our decisions. While in this space some thoughts alternate with others, some ideas develop more than others, and all this happens mechanically, in such a way that in most of the occasions we do not manage to control this mechanism, in such a way that we get used to it and we do nothing to change direction.

February 5, 2020

That which manifests itself in our mind has an influence both inside and outside of us, in what we do, in our language, in our way of relating to others. Everything that settles there always seeks an outlet, somehow. Everything we do belongs first to our mind, it comes from there.

That which acquires a presence in that space begins to develop, it acquires importance as it remains there. It is as if each thought is dedicated to fertilize that ground and with the passage of time begins to bear fruit, which are nothing more than other similar thoughts that grow progressively.

Our mind is like a fertile soil that we dedicate ourselves to sow every day with everything we think about any subject. Each seed remains there, buried, and with the passage of time it begins to sprout, becoming bigger and bigger. We cannot stop this process, because it is part of an automatic system, a mechanism that guides us throughout the day so that, in one way or another, we can survive and solve the various difficulties we have to face every day.

February 6, 2020

The mind guides us when we do not know which direction to take; it contains all the possible alternatives. We only have to wait for the moment when it chooses one of them; then we decide to carry out the action it proposes to us at that instant. We realize that it has indicated to us one alternative out of all the possible ones, and therefore we decide that it is the most indicated for that circumstance or that moment.

Nor do we stop too much to think about the consequences that this particular action may entail. We blindly trust the decision made by our reason. We think that at that moment it is the most beneficial for us and that it will not cause us any harm to act in that way. Only with the passage of time we will see the consequences of acting in that way, so we will draw conclusions from that action and keep that information for later, for when we find ourselves in the future in a similar situation.

Our mind is deciding at each moment what is the best for us, it gives us alternatives and chooses the one it considers most convenient in each circumstance, based on all the information it has previously stored from all the experiences we have had the opportunity to experience.

It perfects itself in this way, through time and the experiences that we have the opportunity to live. It stores all this information in our memory and when we need it, it returns it to our consciousness and makes use of it.

In this way, everything that happens to us becomes valuable information for us, whether that experience has been positive or not. This information is transformed into knowledge, into experience, which we store and which will later serve us to try to solve the different problems that will be happening to us in the future.

These are the contents we use when making decisions, which is why the degree of experience we have is important; whether our decisions are correct or not depends on this.

Our past experience will always be there, we cannot eliminate or change it. It is information that will always remain stored in our memory, waiting to be used at any time.

February 7, 2020

Our development in life and our well-being depend on the functioning of our mind. Everything that is constituted there directs our life in one direction or another.

Our interpretations of reality will mark our path and create our own circumstances. The reading we make of each experience, of the events that happen to us, forms our knowledge of reality and of ourselves.

We can be influenced by an idea that crosses our intellect at a specific moment, in such a way that our mental functioning will depend on that content. This will be reflected in the opinions we have about a given fact, as well as in our own reflections and reasoning. If that idea is wrong or unreasonable, we can easily make a mistake when making a decision or simply when expressing an opinion. But everything starts from there, from a main idea that we have established in our mind and that we continue without realizing that it may be wrong.

And so we can stay for long periods of time, while that idea spreads there and becomes more and more visible in our consciousness.

Only with the passage of time or by some significant experience we may come to realize that this way of thinking is wrong because somehow it is wearing us down, it is destroying us. Then we make the determination not to keep that idea in our head any longer and we look for a different one, another alternative, thanks to which we begin to observe reality from a different point of view.

We are like that; that is how our understanding works. We change over time according to the experiences we go through, based on the interpretations we make of everything that happens to us. In such a way that in all the succession of events that we live through, we change the direction of our own thoughts, our points of view, our opinions.

Over time we build a reality within us that we modify according to our own experiences and the knowledge that we acquire from the outside. This is what makes our life a continuous development, a continuous learning. What is valid for us for a while may not be so valid later on.

This is how we learn; this is how this tool that is our mind is being perfected, learning from each and every one of the experiences we have. This is what creates knowledge and information that is stored in our memory for when we need it.

February 8, 2020

It is difficult to regulate our mind. We move from one situation to another almost without realizing it, so that we are indifferent to the influence that our thoughts are exerting at all times. We have no space to stop and distinguish them. Our mind is like a current that takes us practically wherever it wants.

It is like a land that we are tilling and sowing with thoughts that eventually bear fruit, occupying the space of our consciousness.

We cannot run away from it, since it is the mechanism that enables us to carry out our actions, many of which are necessary for our own survival; it is the one that directs the operations, since it has total control of what we do; it is the one that arranges at all times what we should do, whether it is positive or negative for us.

When we have a purpose in the first place it appears in that space. A purpose is nothing more than a set of thoughts that have been joining together in that place because we are interested in them, because we have found a reason to give importance to that kind of thoughts and not to others. That purpose starts to grow and occupies a space until we finally get down to work: we start to execute behaviors to put it into practice; this is how we conceive our objectives and those things we propose.

First of all, we think about them a lot, to such an extent that all those thoughts spread, they become somehow secured in our mind. With the passage of time all those related thoughts look for an outlet, which in the end is transformed into something that we do outside, in the context closest to us.

When we put into practice all those ideas - previously planned in our mind - but we do not see the result we expect, our mental mechanism starts working again to try to make some changes that may facilitate the achievement of that goal.

Then we try again, implementing new ideas, using

other alternatives. If that goal is very important to us, our intellect will keep working to find the best way to achieve it. It will learn by trial and error the most appropriate way for us to achieve that purpose.

It is also possible that after many attempts we will not be able to reach the proposed goal. In these cases we will feel an enormous frustration, in such a way that our reason will stop looking for alternatives, or at least it will not do it with the same intensity as before. In this way we will gradually abandon this idea over time, we will begin to propose to ourselves other kinds of more achievable goals.

This is how we really work. Over time we change our attention, in such a way that at a certain moment there are things that are very important to us, but with the passage of time and circumstances they cease to be so and are replaced by others. It all depends on where we put the focus of attention at any given moment, although we can spend long periods of time with our attention focused on the same subject, putting aside other things that are also important to us.

Our intellect works in this way: it learns and changes over time. Mental movement is difficult to control: sometimes it goes off and we can hardly stop it. One thought after another begins to emerge and it is very difficult for us to stop this mechanism at that moment. It all depends on the importance we give to each content that arises in our mind at any given moment.

We function in this way, although it is true that we can achieve a certain control over this system, as long as we are aware that this is how it works, that we are conscious of the movement that takes place in this space that is constantly trying to control us.

All this is produced there, within us, within that dimension that is our inner world, which is where our ideas are produced through the thoughts that come from the experiences of the past, which are stored in our memory and are the food of our mind.

February 9, 2020

We have to analyze what consumes us inside. We must carefully observe this mechanism that works at full speed and that propitiates our behaviors.

All the elements that come together in our mind shape our behaviors; we accept them without further ado. We approve of them, even though we sometimes regret them when we see the results of our own actions.

They have the property of being automatic: they do not need a control on our part, a previous reflection. They simply appear there, in our consciousness, suddenly. They follow one after the other, forming sets of contents related to a certain action, to a specific theme, and at the same time they slowly dissolve, while new ones appear naturally, to which we attribute a meaning, an importance, and so on.

Our mental mechanism does not become silent over time, it is constant and influences our state of mind, what we end up being.

Our mind is the place where everything begins. We are accustomed to follow its orders, without caring too much about the consequences that this entails. It is a terrain that surely remains to be explored. If we were to analyze carefully everything that happens in this place, no doubt our actions would be totally different and therefore the effects of our own behaviors would also be different.

Being aware of all this happening is the best tool to concentrate on that space where everything begins, in that space that is actually the beginning of all our behaviors, even our own personality.

Everything that is composed and created there, then leads us towards a certain direction, towards a certain way of thinking; and it also influences our own will, when it comes to making decisions.

All that information stored in our memory causes us to have a certain state of mind at any given moment. Depending on the intensity of those thoughts we feel sad or happy. Everything depends on the tendency of those contents.

Therefore, everything we think has its effect on us, to the extent that we are conscious we will be free of this mechanism, which is rescuing from the deposit of our memory negative and positive aspects of our life, of what we have had the opportunity to live previously.

Our inclination will be to follow each thought that circulates through our consciousness, each thought that is incorporated into our mind, coming from our memory, coming from the past, but we have to learn to gather enough attention to be aware of all that manifests itself within us, that is marking a direction in each of the movements we make in our life. We must get into the habit of slowing down this crazy mechanism.

February 10, 2020

Everything is first formed in our mind and that is marking the way, little by little, slowly. It establishes the direction we must take, at the same time that it elaborates a way of understanding the world, it produces our ideas, our conclusions through mental representations that are manifested and repeated in our consciousness over time.

There is always an abundance of contents in our mind, they are printed there, on the screen of our consciousness. They are articulated, since they are associated with other similar ones. They build ideas, reasonings, reflections from which we cannot separate ourselves. They are spreading more and more, unless we have the ability to stop this mechanism that is getting stronger without us being very conscious of it.

It is like a machine that never stops and we hardly have any tools to defend ourselves against it. All our interpretations of reality are made there, through that mental movement in which a group of thoughts join with other similar ones and give shape to a reality that is only articulated in that space, and that in many occasions has nothing to do with the reality that we find outside, in the ordinary life of external things.

All this content is preserved there for a long time and becomes part of our memory. Sometimes it re-emerges again in that place thanks to this mechanism that triggers elements in our consciousness, coming from the memory of the past; depending on the subject to which we are paying attention at that moment.

Everything is being composed there, in our intellect, at the same time that we act and move through the world. It is like a hidden life that dwells within us and that is the fruit of our own mental mechanism in which thoughts and images that normally tend to be the same, since they are the result of the union with other similar ones, never cease to manifest themselves.

It is a mechanical process that never seems to end, to which we adapt ourselves and do not give it the importance it has. It is a movement that always remains and that feeds our consciousness with contents that many times we do not manage to eliminate, that are expressed there and gain strength as they are repeated, in such a way that they capture our attention, so that we direct our gaze only there and for us that is the only thing that exists in the world.

2. Confusion

February 11, 2020

The chaos, which can sometimes be in our mind, can be quite large, so that it can hinder our perception of things.

Many times we do not find explanations, nor the adequate reasoning, when too much information is agglomerated in our intellect; when in a continuous way they begin to join multiple variables can sow in us the bewilderment, because they are like layers of information of contents that are covering, somehow, the reality.

That is why we sometimes separate ourselves from it, and we settle in a way of seeing the world quite apart from the truth, from what is really happening. There is such a diversity of information that many times we deviate from objectivity, from the true reality, and we start to think things without foundation, so that we can live in deception for long periods of time.

We are not rigorous when it comes to handling all those elements that appear there, when they are abundant. We do not have enough capacity to manage them properly and we build a mental structure that is not safe, because we always opt for the first thing that comes to our mind, for all those thoughts that constantly surround us and that make us see reality in a certain way. It is only with time that we discover that the world is different. The experiences we go through help us to distinguish the true reality.

Therefore, many thoughts that occupy our reason, that remain there, suspended for long periods of time managing to conquer our attention, may not conform to the truth; although they remain as images that are illuminated in our consciousness and rise one above the other, forcing us to pigeonhole what we observe.

We get used to all those frequent thoughts because they are the most active in those moments and we do not get used to empty our mind of all those constant reproductions that grow and expand with the passage of time.

Everything that manifests in our consciousness has an extraordinary influence on us, so that it makes us experience a series of emotions, as our thoughts manifest. Every fact, every event has an enormous impact on us.

We cannot run away from this mechanism, but if we examine it and get to know how it works, we can moderate it in some way. If we know its characteristics and examine the processes that take place in that space and that build our particular way of understanding reality, we can have a very powerful tool to understand ourselves; to correct all that confusion, all that disorder that in many occasions we experience due to the lack of knowledge of our own mental mechanism.

February 12, 2020

Our mind is a great instrument that can help us if we use it properly. It can also become, on the contrary, our main enemy if we fail to clean all those toxic and negative thoughts that often accumulate without us being aware of it.

Everything depends on the quality of the representations that we have there at any given moment. If they are positive, we will be on the right path; if they divert us from what we are, in the end we will live on the path of suffering for a long period of time, until we realize what is hurting us, which is usually a certain way of thinking that we create without realizing it through a series of specific thoughts that do not suit us, that have arisen there and that have been repeated because we have paid attention to them.

Problems arise mainly from maintaining a series of thoughts over time. They do not have so much influence on us if they only occupy a brief space of time, if we let them pass by without giving them importance. When they begin to have a great effect on us is when they take root because we pay excessive attention to them. Then we cannot get rid of them, we have great difficulty in eliminating them.

All those who know themselves and who are aware that this is so, try to make an effort so that certain negative contents do not continue to grow in their mind. That is why in them there is no confusion, disorder. And it is because they have achieved a certain control over themselves, over what they think and how they think. They have discovered the consequences of thinking and acting in a certain way, and they have done so through the experiences they have lived throughout their lives. All of this has been a learning experience for them, so they are not so easily manipulated by a certain thought or idea.

February 13, 2020

We are always in the company of our mind; we cannot close the door on it; even if, with a little effort on our part, we manage not to let it have so much impact on us.

A thought, however small it may be, can have a great influence, since it can attract other small thoughts that can unite and form in this way a set of contents that can lead us to a determined action. Then these thoughts spread, in such a way that they favor the appearance of other similar thoughts and thus compose the direction in which we move.

We must bear in mind that each thought can have an intention, and if it is a set of similar thoughts, its intention will be stronger, it will influence us much more.

Our mind is populated with sets of thoughts that influence us during a determined period. They transmit to us what we should do and infect our reason with a way of understanding reality. Little by little they make their way into our consciousness when we observe ourselves and look inside ourselves to see what we are thinking at that moment.

In our mind is first transmitted what we are going to do later, so it is vital that we begin to take into account what we think most often, because that will determine our subsequent behaviors.

Each thing we think has an effect on us, in one way or another. It determines us without us being aware of it many times. They are contents that grow as we pay attention to them, in such a way that they are triggered and increase until they completely take over our attention.

They make us waste a lot of time and energy, especially when they are thoughts that do not lead anywhere, that are not really useful. When the number of similar thoughts is too many, we can spend long periods of time focused on a single subject, completely dominated by a series of ideas that capture all our attention. In these cases we are only attentive to those specific thoughts, which manifest themselves over and over again, repeatedly, in that space.

In this way, a vicious circle is formed within us that slowly weaves itself until it begins to grow larger and larger, until it reaches a point of difficult return. We can be entangled in absurd ideas, which serve no purpose, for long periods of time. When we realize that we are making a mistake, it is sometimes quite difficult to turn back, to restart.

The movement of our mind is like that, it works this way. The problem is that we are not the ones who have the initiative; sometimes we lack the will to stop this automatic system that is determining us, leading us in a direction that sometimes is not what we really want.

Our suffering comes from there, it comes from this way of functioning that we have; it is the result of a great number of negative thoughts about life, about ourselves, which are joined together until they form a totally closed negative mental structure, which cannot enter to modify it.

February 15, 2020

When we suffer alterations or are in a situation of internal conflict, it is because a series of thoughts have taken over our mind and have spread throughout our consciousness. In these cases it is advisable that we replace some thoughts with others. Until we make that effort, those thoughts will not disappear and will become stronger as time goes by.

To make this change we must put the focus of attention on those contents where we think that the solution to our problem can be found. From then on we must focus more on those contents, on those kinds of thoughts and not on others, until they gradually expand in our mind and replace the existing ones.

The mastery of the mind is based on this: there are a series of thoughts that manage to take control of the mental movement because they have established themselves there by being the most repeated for some reason. When these thoughts, which are more deeply rooted and which dominate and control the mental processes, begin to be replaced by others, then they gradually lose their power and influence.

In our intellect, therefore, there is a game of thoughts that try to take control; and they try to achieve it by extending more and more, trying to repeat themselves and associating with other similar thoughts to increase their strength and dominance.

In this mental game we can participate in a voluntary way, when we consciously change the focus of attention, when we manifest our interest towards some kind of concrete contents. Then this has an effect on our mind, which immediately stops giving prominence to the thoughts that at that moment are there and tries to look for other kinds of different elements more related to the subject that at that moment is interesting us.

This process has as a consequence a change, in the sense that some thoughts that were dominating in a certain moment the mental space begin to diminish their intensity so that other different ones occupy their place. This is the reason why in many occasions we can change our mind, see the same reality in a different way: it is because our thoughts are changing, they are changing with time and circumstances. Those contents that dominate that space can cease to do so in a very short time, simply because we divert our attention to a different place.

In our mind this game is established, which is a game of dominance of some thoughts over others. Those that have more strength are the ones that manage to win, they are the ones that end up establishing themselves in our consciousness and are the ones that capture our attention, so that they force us to go in a certain direction.

When we spend long periods of time obsessed by some matter that worries us, in reality what is taking place is this mental game, this game of domination of some thoughts over others. When we always think about the same thing it is because some thoughts have become established, have gained strength and will not stop repeating themselves until unconsciously or voluntarily there is a change of content, a change in the focus of attention to another kind of different thoughts.

February 16, 2020

We produce lots and lots of ideas all day long. Our mind is like a machine that never stops producing, it is as if it cannot be stopped. In it, thoughts follow one after the other in a mechanical way, we only notice those that call our attention for some reason, then we focus on them and from then on they start to multiply suddenly.

It is a movement that we can hardly stop, so that our ideas become larger as we go deeper into them, as we stop at a particular point because it has some importance for us. In this way, images and thoughts do not cease to be exposed, and they are leading themselves by themselves, without the participation of our will, of our true desires.

It is like a blank sheet of paper that at every moment tries to fill itself with contents and elements that occupy that space, until others emerge that eliminate those that already exist and take their place. Our intellect is like a sheet of paper that never finishes writing itself, it is always overwriting itself in a movement that seems to have no end.

It is a movement that consists of a multitude of elements that are triggered from the depths of our memory and that we barely have the capacity to stop, to reach a control over it. It is like a river that carries us along, like a current that is always running and that we cannot regulate.

It is important that we keep this in mind because it is the first thing we have to be aware of. In this way we will find many explanations to our acts, to our unconscious actions. We have to understand that in many occasions we limit ourselves to obey this mechanical and uncontrolled movement that takes place in that space and that tries to lead us towards a certain direction.

Everything we do belongs, in the first place, to that movement, it starts from there. Everything is first represented in our mind before it becomes part of our behavior on the outside. Everything is first formed there, in that space where our thoughts are represented and the path to follow is established.

It is a mechanism that somehow determines us. If we understand this in this way, we will find the causes of many of our conflicts, of our suffering and of all our negativity, which often pushes us to stop acting, especially when it has been cultivated for a long time within us.

This forces us to stop and study in more depth this mechanism that at first seems inflexible, because it is very difficult to control.

February 18, 2020

This system, which is necessary for our own survival and can become beneficial in many cases, can sometimes be harmful, to the extent that it forces us to behave automatically, as if we were a robot, causing a series of behaviors that then become habits that are not good for us.

Everything depends on what is produced in our mind, on the elements that are part of that movement that in many occasions is difficult to stop; it depends on the contents that are established there. If they are beneficial for us we will not have any problem, but if they are harmful elements, toxic thoughts, this will lead us to suffering, to create in us a negative atmosphere that will contaminate everything: every thought we have afterwards and every behavior we perform.

If we use negative thoughts, our inner speech, that inner dialogue that we have with ourselves, will also be affected and therefore will be negative, and this will influence us in our inner conversations that we have with ourselves about any fact, any situation that we live in every moment.

Our mind is always with us. Depending on the kind of thoughts we have, so will be our mood in every situation, our vision of the world, of others. That is why this process that takes place within us is so important, acting constantly in a never-ending movement that determines us in some way, because it has the power to lead our actions and to incline our own thoughts in a specific direction.

February 20, 2020

Every time you look at yourself you discover something new. If you search a little inside yourself, you will realize how all those mental manifestations that arise in your consciousness are constructed and that generate a certain way of thinking that changes with the passage of time.

All these manifestations come from the register of your memory. They are contents that have penetrated you through each and every one of the experiences that you have had the opportunity to experience throughout your life.

These elements that are found in your memory, later emerge in your consciousness, many times in a disorganized way, without a concrete order, and they are exposed there, in such a way that they force you to pay attention to them.

When these thoughts gain strength, when they try to unite with each other, they remain and establish themselves there for long periods of time, creating a whole series of ideas that little by little manifest themselves in your mind and that compose a structure of contents that later will be difficult to eliminate.

Throughout the day we think about a multitude of things, extol many memories and give importance to a series of specific thoughts. In this way we allow them to grow in this space without often being aware of the consequences of this multiplicity of thoughts to which we pay exaggerated attention.

When we find ourselves in all this amplitude and we are conscious of the influence that all these impressions have, we can find the way so that all these representations, in the form of thoughts, do not end up taking hold of us.

If we observe this properly, we can easily detect those irrational thoughts that we often invent in order to fantasize or imagine a reality different from the one we really find outside.

Our intellect facilitates this possibility: that of dispensing with the real world, passing to an imaginative state where we can overcome the reality that surrounds us, considering another alternative world to the existing one, in which we find ourselves with a greater number of possibilities, although everything is a product of our own imagination.

Sometimes, when we do not find answers in the world around us or we are faced with something that we think is unattainable, in the end we end up inventing another new reality through the use of our own mind, giving importance to everything that may arise in those moments from our imagination. We leave aside objectivity, our rational part, and we abandon ourselves to a false illusion for long periods of time; all this leads us to walk along uncertain paths.

February 21, 2020

Our mind works very fast. When it is irrational we cannot stop it, for it is inclined to repeat over and over again a series of thoughts that we cannot control, that are not logical and that make us have a wrong vision of things.

In those moments we need a bit of enlightenment, of clarity, to find the possibilities of guessing a way out of that darkness that hovers over us in those moments. Sometimes we do not find it in those moments, so that we remain involved in a vicious circle of irrational ideas that go nowhere.

That is when we need to find a way out of that trap, of that deception to which our reason submits us. It is dangerous for our mind to be filled with erroneous thoughts, with false thoughts, because this will provoke a movement in us that will lead us to carry out irrational acts; all this will have a reflection in our external behaviors.

If we embark for a long time in an irrational world, which has nothing to do with reality, we will be destined to fail. That is why we must be attentive to everything that is built in that space and we must not accommodate ourselves to that world that in many occasions is proposed to us, since sometimes it has nothing to do with reality.

This is important to keep in mind because everything that starts there then has a reflection in what we do or do not do; everything has a correspondence. If we live in an illusory world, in the end this will have consequences for us, which we will see over time.

February 22, 2020

Our inner universe is very large, it is difficult to locate the information, to try to get the one we need at every moment to resolve all conflicts.

Our intellectual capacity allows us to have a certain alacrity at the time of relating one information with another, but our mind is so wide that in many occasions we cannot control that game where many thoughts are conducted without a determined direction, in such a way that in those moments our mind becomes a land populated with elements that circulate without order, without a determined direction.

In those moments is when we feel that there is conflict within us, we are aware that at that moment we are facing a difficulty.

Our problems have their origin there, in that space; they start first from within us, they are the result of the conflict that is established between some thoughts and others, when we do not find the appropriate information to solve a difficulty.

The mind goes very fast; it constantly deceives us; it hides information from us sometimes, when we need it most; it can instill fear in us; it can darken our future: when we do not find a way out, when there is no place in our consciousness where we can find a way out.

Often we just go along with it; no matter what the issue is, we depend on every thought that arises in it, we just follow it.

We remain immobile when thoughts begin to arise, when thoughts begin to be added there and are joining each other, while we continue walking following this mental movement that contains each step we must take, because each thought is placed one after another in our consciousness, following a specific order; it is as if this mechanism took possession of us, as a circular game that begins and ends always in the same place.

Sometimes we become confused, since we carry out behaviors with which we do not agree, simply because we have tolerated certain ideas, certain thoughts, because we have allowed them to occur without further ado. This leads us inevitably to act in a particular way, because those thoughts have been repeated so much in our consciousness that we have become accustomed to them; they have made us act in a certain way.

This is why we often feel confused and have the feeling that there is no order. Sometimes we feel blocked for this reason: it is like the current of a river that sometimes stagnates and does not flow; it remains concentrated in the same thoughts that begin to gain strength.

For this same reason, because they are always the same and are repeated over and over again, sometimes we do not find a way out, we feel that something is confusing us, that within us there is something that is irritating us, that is creating confusion and conflict: they are nothing more than the contents that at that moment are being represented in that space, that are creating disorder and confusion.

February 23, 2020

Everything is built there, in our mind. We are always accompanied by it, wherever we go. It always tries to take us by the current that is created little by little, with each thought that is dragged along the consciousness.

We can also create new ideas, new reasoning, when we try to unite some thoughts with others, when we use our logic we build other forms of thought that take shape, a structure.

We are building, in this way, a way of thinking that we can maintain for long periods of time, because we cultivate it without realizing it, until one day something changes and we modify that way of thinking, because another series of new thoughts begin to mix and create another new structure that begins to mark a new tendency.

Then we begin to see reality in a different way from how we have seen it before, because in our mind begins to promote another kind of different thoughts.

Over time, different ways of understanding the world are formed. Sometimes these can become contradictory, which sow in us a great restlessness, because we see that in our mind move contrary thoughts and we do not know which one to choose; we do not know how to find the truth or a good foundation.

Sometimes, all these contents are integrated without a determined order, which creates confusion in those moments. We do not know how to express what we are thinking, or where we want to go; this happens frequently.

This confusion can take us away from reality, because we do not reach clarity. In those moments, a conflict begins to build within us and grows within the terrain of our consciousness. Then we do not find ourselves, we do not find the exact words to designate what is happening to us at that moment.

The more we try to fight that situation, the more it spreads within us. It is as if certain thoughts reinforce themselves automatically and independently, once they have managed to settle there.

When all these pieces come together they create within us a disorderly mixture of confused thoughts from which we cannot escape, although we can explore and discover what thoughts are sowing our confusion, what is propitiating this mental movement that leads us to confusion and that is creating restlessness in those moments.

We will soon become aware of the kind of contents that are being established. In those moments we will realize the dimension they have and the influence they exert on us. We will notice that there are many similar thoughts that are difficult to manage, because they appear and fade very quickly across the entire surface of our consciousness.

February 24, 2020

The destination of our thoughts is the mind; they tend to arise in our consciousness, to circulate through it. Sometimes they anticipate our intentions, since on many occasions we think things that do not correspond many times.

They are contradictory contents, contrary to what we really want to do. They are occupying a place there and are forming a line of action, they are serving us to carry out actions in our closest context.

When we have a behavior what we do is nothing more than applying what we are thinking at that moment, what exists in our intellect at that moment. The characteristics of our behavior depend on that, on the content that at that moment is in our consciousness, which after so much persistence, after so much repetition, has come to form a structure of elements so strong that we feel obliged to replicate it in reality, to convert it into action, even if that action is contradictory to other actions that we have performed previously. At that moment we do not try to fight that contradiction, but we simply tend to perform that behavior, even if it is contrary to what we usually think.

In many occasions we deny reality because our mind is full of contradictions that are presented one after another through our thoughts. Sometimes we cannot avoid that our thoughts have a certain tendency and that they build, without hardly realizing it, a way of understanding reality in a specific way.

February 25, 2020

Many times we want to find answers to many doubts that we have, but no matter how much we reflect we do not find in many occasions a convincing and reasonable explanation to many unknowns that life poses to us. Perhaps we have too much information inside, in our memory, and that is why we may find it difficult to find the data we need to solve all those doubts.

The information we have is hidden information, it is information that we have acquired over time, from our own experiences throughout our lives, but it does not appear so easily when we need it. Much of this information can only emerge through quiet reflection, when we are calm and alone with ourselves and we ask ourselves questions and try to find the answers in a calm way, without any hurry and without forcing anything. Then the answers that we need to clarify all those doubts that life poses to us come to us.

Not always the information that we need manifests itself in our mind, in many occasions an information arises that diverts us from the direction in which we intend to go. There is so much information that we have inside that many times some contents arise in our consciousness that have nothing to do with what we need to know at that moment, with the explanations we are looking for and with the reasoning we are trying to do.

That is why it is easy for us to lose concentration many times when we focus on a certain subject. It is easy for us to get diverted to other kinds of thoughts that have nothing to do with that subject. Our mind is a difficult mechanism to manage; it works by impulses and it is frequent that we change our activity easily, that we go from one action to another different one. All this is due to this movement, which is very dynamic and sometimes contradictory, in such a way that we can have one thought and the opposite in a very short space of time.

We must also fight against this if we want a certain order to be produced in that space and not have so many contradictions. Just knowing that this can happen is already an important step; it is something that can help us to transform our model of thinking, our way of reflecting on those things that happen to us.

February 26, 2020

If we look at it, in our mind there is always a great variety of ideas, contents, images and many elements that are known to us, that are familiar to us. Even if they pass by in a transitory way they have been filling the gap in our memory for many years, and that is why they are known to us; they have strength when they come up to our consciousness.

They are contents with which we have previously had some experience, in some form. They are images that we have seen before. All these elements are familiar to us, we know where they come from. They are like ingredients that are added to each other and when they come together they attract our attention, and therefore they consume our time, because we are aware of them practically most of the time.

We give them importance and that is why they quickly begin to spread from one end of our consciousness to the other; they occupy all that space.

Sometimes they do it without a concrete order, following the current of an idea, of a thought, in a movement that seems to have no end, because it never diminishes, unless we look away from those thoughts and our attention is fixed on other things that are outside. Then other contents occupy that place, in such a way that another reality begins to be articulated, different from the one that was there before.

February 27, 2020

In our mind there is a lot of material, but much of all that information is disordered, it is only ordered a little when it arises there, when we put our focus of attention on it and we order certain ideas, when we try to reason about a particular issue. All the information we have is ordered when it appears in that space, although much of that information appears suddenly, in an unexpected way many times.

When it does not manage to be ordered and that disorder extends over time, then we fall into confusion. In those moments is when we do not know how to act, what option to choose or what direction to take. We do not manage to order what appears disordered. Surely in those moments there is information that we need but that does not appear, that is hidden or that has not yet emerged in our consciousness. It is as if we lack elements to think clearly. In those moments we do not know very well how to act and we let ourselves be carried away by the current of all those disordered and confused thoughts that at that moment dominate us.

Those are the moments in which we feel that there is a confusion in us, and until we do not solve it we feel a great restlessness, we feel insecure, we do not become fully aware of our actions. We act like a robot, like a puppet that lets itself be carried away by what our intellect dictates to us at any given moment.

In these cases is when we need to be more conscious to stop that mental movement that tries to dominate us. We must observe ourselves to realize what kind of thoughts are driving us. It is the only way to re-establish that lost order: that mental balance that we need so that there is logic in our thinking, in our way of reasoning and understanding the world.

March 1, 2020

In our mind there is usually disorder, there is always a series of elements that do not relate well. We need a bit of ingenuity to order those contents and thus solve many confusions that are only created there, that we only create ourselves.

It is difficult for us to decompose all that mental structure that we have been building over time and that is increasingly extended as we always put our focus of attention on specific thoughts.

Sometimes we reach despair when we cannot solve a difficulty, solve a problem we have at that moment. We do not know how to manage the information that our reason gives us, we do not know how to put aside those elements that are not useful to solve that problem. Many times we let time be the one that provides us with an alternative to be able to get out of that difficulty.

Many times a darkness spreads that we do not know how to interrupt. This happens when we only keep a series of negative, toxic thoughts that prevent us from moving forward, that only create disorder and confusion within us. When there is only this kind of thoughts we feel disoriented, we do not know how to find a convincing explanation to what is happening to us. Life just happens, without us being able to do anything to stop acting in a certain way that is surely harming us.

In those moments we are possessed by a vicious circle that is in charge of thinking for ourselves, that exerts an enormous power of such magnitude that we can hardly do anything to get rid of it, to annul its effect.

We only limit ourselves to act determined by its influence. Although we are aware that this happens, we let ourselves be carried away by inertia, we do nothing to avoid it. In these cases we act as if we were a robot that follows a mental programming that we ourselves have been developing over time, through a series of repetitive habits that have become stronger and stronger within us.

March 2, 2020

In the play of the mind a series of contents are related, thus generating, in this way, a new knowledge for us. Our consciousness is like a blank screen that is filled with images that take shape according to the thoughts that arise automatically from our memory.

These thoughts are linked to each other according to a series of conditions and at the same time they dissolve. Our opinions, our points of view, our will, depend on how these thoughts are formed; on the direction they take.

If the composition of those thoughts that are formed there has a negative tendency, this will influence the way we see the world at that moment; this will place us in a negative terrain, so that our vision of reality will also be influenced by this.

Some of them we manage to put aside because we consider them negative for us, but others remain there and it is complicated to get rid of them, because they take root so strongly, based on repetition, that it is not so easy to eliminate them.

They are very clearly distinguishable, since they stand out, since they are those thoughts to which we pay attention. They gain great strength and become the main ones in our consciousness. Their presence in it dilates, widens with time. They are increasing, since they are joining with other similar ones, with others closer, in such a way that our mind tends to focus on that kind of thoughts and not on others.

Everything is a function of the way in which these contents are administered. A mental structure is created, composed of our own thoughts, which conditions us in some way; it sows a certain vision of things.

March 3, 2020

What happens to us is like an apprenticeship for us, it is information that in the end is stored in our memory.

Apart from this, in our mind we build our own subjective version of what we see outside. In such a way that we draw our own conclusions and that information finally remains stored as a memory that with time can emerge again to our conscience.

In many occasions we are not objective with respect to the external reality, we always have our own point of view of what happens, of the events that happen to us daily. Everyone has their own version of the facts, it is as if we perceive reality differently from each other. We often try to adapt the external reality to our point of view, to try to accommodate what happens outside with our own thoughts that we have at that moment.

In this way, on many occasions, we create a reality inside ourselves that differs from what exists outside, from what is happening on the outside. There is, in these cases, no similarity between what we think and what is happening outside of us.

Our thoughts, in this sense, can become very subjective, for they try to accommodate our own tastes, our most frequent opinions about certain subjects. We have an intellect that tries to adapt to what we have been thinking habitually and we cannot get it out of there, we cannot get it to work differently overnight.

That is why it is difficult, many times, to change our opinion, our personal point of view, which has some concrete ideas and it is very difficult that in a short space of time they change, that we begin to think the opposite, unless we experience an extraordinary situation that forces us to rethink our own ideas.

All this leads us to think that in our mind moves a set of thoughts that often follow the same line, that always go in a direction that with the passage of time is difficult to change: to achieve a vision contrary to the one we have been holding previously.

It seems that significant changes only occur when something important happens to us, some vital experience that makes us rethink many things, so that in these cases we begin to give importance to other issues that previously remained in oblivion. In such cases many thoughts that normally used to haunt that space begin to be repeated less frequently, until they disappear. This is how we function inside, this is the movement of our mind.

When we are negative, it actually happens because of this. It is because we have dedicated ourselves to fill our brain with toxic thoughts and we have habituated it to work that way, to go in that direction. That is why it is so difficult to change habits, because we have trained our mind to act with a specific intention, with thoughts that are hurting us without us being very aware of it. We, in front of this, do not give importance to it, because it seems that this is the normal thing, while a series of thoughts that do not do us any good are repeated over and over again.

When we become aware of this and we want to change this tendency, it is very difficult for us to achieve it. We have insisted so much on these kinds of negative thoughts that in the end we have created within us a mental structure that always tries to lead us in the same direction and it is very difficult for us to change from one day to the next.

March 4, 2020

We all use a large number of thoughts on a daily basis, although it is true that many of them are repeated. Within all those thoughts that we repeat, the proportion of negative thoughts is also very high: our mind tends internally to repeat negative toxic thoughts that are not good for us. This leads us to have a negative vision of life, of those things that we could do and that we do not do because of our mental system.

Our negativity is a ball that we are dragging full of thoughts that as we move it gets bigger and bigger and we cannot stop it, in any way. All this breaks our inner harmony, because this ball of thoughts is gaining more and more strength and is rushing until it is established in us a negative view of life.

Our mind can be filled with darkness if we do not act in time. Everything depends on the contents that at that moment are occupying the consciousness. They can be instruments loaded with a great negativity and we must inhibit them in some way, to get out of that hard darkness that sometimes expands through our mind and overwhelms us without us being very conscious of it.

Negativity can settle inside us, it can fill our consciousness with toxic thoughts, so that we can build a quite negative vision of reality that can then harm us when making decisions, in our own actions and behaviors. Negative thoughts are the seed of a negative attitude, of a state of mind where anguish, sadness and restlessness can reign.

This only occurs if we enter into that game of the mind, if we fail to stop that system, that movement that is like a vicious circle that turns endlessly returning always to the same starting point.

All this happens because we pay attention to a certain set of thoughts; then these are triggered, they begin to emerge more and more strongly, in a movement in which they will begin to repeat themselves over and over again, joining with other similar thoughts, until they manage to impose a reality that sometimes does not correspond to the one we find outside, in the world around us.

March 5, 2020

The mind, in reality, expresses what is important to us at any given moment. Relevant contents then begin to rise on that matter, until we fix our attention on different ones, on other things. From then on, our mental movement changes, there is an alternation of thoughts depending on where we place our focus of attention at any given moment.

Sometimes, depending on the circumstances, we are inclined to spend a long time on the same thoughts. This has a great impact on us, since the thoughts corresponding to that particular subject are spreading there and become strong, in such a way that they are mixed with other similar contents and occupy a large space; this happens when we do not stop thinking about a certain subject.

Although we have the capacity to change the orientation of our thoughts, many times we allow them to capture us. Then we begin to build a reality, an alternative world, because we enter into that game: in which each thought is like a seed that we plant and begins to grow every time that thought appears, at the same time that other thoughts begin to hide.

Everything is part of that movement that is really the one that manufactures our internal reality: that reality that only exists in that space and that in many occasions has nothing to do with the one outside.

Your mind can transport you to the past or to the future, depending on the direction your thoughts take. There, opinions are formed that lead you to have a specific point of view on an issue. It imprints a series of conclusions that are manufactured with each content that emerges from your memory: they are reflections that are produced one after another that help you understand the world around you and make the decisions you need at a given time.

Your mind also learns from every event that happens to you, it draws its own conclusions by accumulating all the information that comes to it from outside. It joins it with other similar information that you already have in your memory and in this way you create a point of view about what you are observing, what you have in front of you; depending on the situation in which you are at that moment, it will act in one way or another.

It is the place where everything is created beforehand. It is where all the loose ends come together and where we create our own vision of things, which sometimes does not correspond to what is really happening: there may be contradictions in our way of thinking that later, with time, we may become aware of them.

Sometimes there is a big difference between our own reality and the one we build inside us, which grows with the passage of time according to those thoughts that spread from our memory.

Sometimes we create impossible, imaginary worlds, which only exist there and have nothing to do with the real world, with which we have contact when we go out in the street and observe others, when we relate to the people around us.

All this is the result of our own imagination, of our mental functioning, which often encourages us to build a parallel world to escape, even for a short period of time, from the world in which we live, which is often not as pleasant as we would like it to be. Sometimes we feel the need to use our reason to leave aside our own conflicts, our suffering, and that is why we elaborate another, more pleasant reality that only has pleasant effects for us.

It is a way of escaping from the reality in which we live, which in many occasions only throws stones at us, so that we do not find the way to solve our problems.

Sometimes there are sudden changes in that space, and it is due to all this, to that mental movement that constantly takes us from one reality to another: from a reality that only exists in our own imagination to the one that truly exists outside, in the world that surrounds us, in the external world.

March 6, 2020

In our mind there is sometimes a great deception. We imagine things that then do not exist in reality or we invent reasons to justify a certain behavior. Many times we have thoughts without any logic, simply because at that moment we are interested in having that kind of thoughts for some reason.

If we pay attention to what is in that space, we will see that we often insist on creating a world outside reality. We come to live in fantasy for some periods of time, believing that the real world is the one we are imagining there. Only with the passage of time do we realize that this is not so, until reality puts us in our place.

Our mind is a space where we can create a parallel world, an imaginary world, which only exists in our imagination. We can live for a long time oblivious to reality, to what is happening outside, in our closest context. And it is because in those moments we follow the dictates of our intellect, which makes us believe in a different world, totally unreal, that has nothing to do with the reality that exists outside: in the world where most people live.

The mind behaves in this way because it is much more comfortable for it to move in a world invented to suit our desires. When we live in a parallel reality, where we have hardly any problems and do not encounter difficulties of any kind, we feel that life is much more comfortable for us. Moreover, living in this other parallel world means that we do not have to face the problems of everyday life, that we are not aware of suffering and all those things that can cause us emotional pain.

When we live far from reality, as if we were in a parallel world, we have to remember that it may be for some of these reasons. We will verify with time that living far away from the reality that surrounds us, can be quite harmful for us, because we come to have a wrong vision of things. We can give importance to certain things that have no use, that have no value.

If we live permanently in an imaginary world, we put aside, without realizing it, the things that are really important in life. We can lose our energy in matters that serve no purpose. And this can go on for a long time, depending on our level of imagination, until one day we get a reality check and realize that the invented world in which we live has nothing to do with the real world, in which the people we know and most of those around us live.

That is when we try to make an effort to return to reality, leaving aside our fantasies and all that world created only in our imagination. Only at that moment will other kinds of contents begin to manifest in our mind that are more adjusted to the world in which we live. In those instants we begin to be more realistic, to realize all the manipulation that the mind has exerted on us.

In those moments we are aware that we have allowed ourselves to be manipulated because deep down it was convenient for us, to escape from reality because we felt that need, surely to escape from our problems by creating a world within us that is friendlier and with fewer difficulties. These are the most frequent reasons why we often turn to our imagination, to invent a parallel reality in which there is no problem, or in which we do not find any setback and everything happens as we imagine it.

There are people who live for long periods of time in their fantasy world, in their unreal world. We can detect it clearly when they are in front of us and they express themselves and tell us something of their life, of what they do, of what they think. It is easy to detect if that person is in reality or is a little lost in matters that have nothing to do with the present moment, with the world in which we live.

3. Observation

March 8, 2020

We must organize ourselves a little better inside. It is not easy because there is a lot of information that is hidden, that does not appear when we need it most. We limit ourselves to obtain only a few data from all the information that appears in our mind, but we must take into account that there is other information that is hidden and that could also be of interest to us to solve any question at any given time.

We can only limit ourselves to the information that appears little by little in our consciousness, which is filled with data that are stored in our memory and others that are the result of the analysis and reflection that we do at each moment with all those elements that we have at each moment.

If we are in the habit of observing ourselves, we will find it very easy to discover that information that is often hidden from us. We only need to have a little patience and wait for it to emerge little by little to give an answer to everything we need to know to survive in every moment.

If we use the mind in this way it becomes a great tool to face the difficulties that we have to live. We only need to be a little observant and have very clear ideas about how we work inside. If we know that all this information can influence and dominate us to the point of forcing us to go in a specific direction, we can achieve a certain control over ourselves and organize our inner world a little better.

If we achieve this we can then see the consequences on the outside, in our way of being in the world, in our way of relating and observing the reality that surrounds us at every moment.

March 9, 2020

When many similar thoughts come together and begin to register one after another in our consciousness, it is as if we have no way out, as if they are imprinted there and there is no way to get rid of them, to think of something else. We seem to be incapable of ending that movement in these cases.

When this occurs, when we have this sensation, we should make an effort to level up, to stop and observe carefully how that mental movement is affecting our state of mind. We should make an effort to place ourselves at another, slightly higher level. In this way we could read on the screen of our consciousness everything that is happening within us. In this way we could establish a certain order; we could realize which thoughts are having an effect on us, or which ideas are contradictory.

This exercise of trying to be above our intellect in moments of conflict, of mental confusion, we can use it as a valid instrument, as a tool that will give us the capacity to establish a certain order.

We only have to raise our level of attention a little and look inside, in this way we will glimpse everything that is happening inside us: how one thought is being linked to another and how our mind tries to trap us, to deceive us, drawing a very different reality that in most cases does not correspond with the one we find in the real world, with the one we find outside.

Then, somehow, those thoughts begin to annul themselves, to dissolve easily, in a natural way, without us having to make a major effort on our part. We will see that what was confusing us one day, that was generating an internal conflict, begins to deviate and fade away, and that at the same time other kinds of thoughts different from those that were trying to confuse us begin to come to light. We will observe that the toxic thoughts disappear little by little.

Just by the mere fact of having raised our level of attention, of observation, by having placed ourselves a little further, above our mind, in these cases, we will see that the mental trap in which we were trapped no longer has an effect on us.

When this happens it is because we change our mental situation to one that is more favorable to us. The conflicts disappear, the difficulties at a mental level because we have changed the kind of thoughts, and this has different consequences: what was oppressing us stops doing so. It is as if another different space opens up, with another kind of contents that begin to develop, the same as the previous ones, and they begin to penetrate more and more into our consciousness and to unite with other similar ones, until we reach another way of understanding things, another different vision of the world; this is how this mechanism works.

It is the way to put an end to our suffering, to that which disturbs us, to that which causes us confusion. Everything has a cause first in this space: thoughts that determine us without us being aware of it, that are constantly reproduced in our consciousness and that represent a certain vision of things.

March 11, 2020

Our mind is what, in reality, determines us; it is what is the basis for all our actions. That is why we should be interested in observing all those representations that are installed in our consciousness, especially those that are repeated more frequently; all these contents belong to our memory. They are the result of past activity; they belong to us, and that is why we must be able to control all those elements that often influence our mental balance.

And the fact is that we get used to this functioning, to this way we have of working inside. The opposite would mean to make an effort on our part and we are not always willing to do it, so in many occasions we allow that which weakens us to settle for long periods of time in our consciousness, and in the end we end up subject to that kind of contents that gain strength and become main, influencing our way of expressing ourselves, in our way of speaking, in our system of thought, in the way we see and consider everything that happens to us.

Our mind is an instrument that is in constant movement, that is always working and shaping our way of seeing the world at every moment. It is inclining us in a certain direction, depending on the thoughts we have at any given moment.

It is therefore important to pay attention and to know its properties. It is an instrument that we should know in more detail. If we know how it works, if we understand that its tendency is to repeat almost always the same thoughts until they become firm in our consciousness, we will come to understand its effects on us.

If we learn to properly manage our own mental system and many of the movements that occur there, we will come to have benefits on our own life, on our moods.

We only need to be able to observe how thoughts follow one after another; to observe all those images that appear in our consciousness. Just by paying attention to all these internal elements that struggle to gain a foothold, we can achieve a certain control and somehow weaken the influence that it exerts on us.

Its effects will be different, but for that we have to get used to live in that terrain where our beliefs, our ideas are produced, where our behaviors and our actions originate.

It is enough for us to reduce its influence on us, so that those thoughts that are harmful do not become bigger with time, so that they do not increase when they are joined with other similar thoughts. If we achieve this, our sensations will be very different and our actions will also be influenced by this other form of consciousness.

March 12, 2020

It is important to make a careful analysis of what is repeated in our mind most of the time. It is there, in all that variety of thoughts, where we will find the keys of everything that happens to us, of our current situation and of all those things that we have done before.

Everything that is represented there then has a consequence outside, in our life.

We must observe the movement of our intellect, of our habitual thoughts, because that is where everything begins. If they are negative we must find out the reason, which will surely be in the importance we have given to that particular kind of thoughts. We cannot get hooked to that kind of thoughts, to some ideas, if they are harmful to us; and we can easily detect that if we notice that those kinds of contents are established most of the time in that place.

If we really want to feel free we must have the habit of observing ourselves, to detect the quality of our own thoughts, of what they mean to us; it is the best tool to face the power that our own mind has over us. It is the best way to clean our own consciousness of negative contents.

In this way it is likely that where there is darkness we will find clarity; it is the only possible way. It is there where we must focus our energy and attention, in all those expressions that are produced in that space and that move us from one place to another without us often being aware of it.

In this way we will see how some thoughts are expanding trying to quickly capture our attention. We will become aware of all this. We will be aware that the current state of our situation is the result of all that we have previously thought, of all that has previously passed through our consciousness.

With this system we can manage to put aside in some way those contents that harm us: those thoughts that try to hurt us, especially those that are loaded with negativity.

March 13, 2020

We cannot let ourselves be carried away by our habits, which are nothing more than a consequence of what our mind dictates to us at every moment, because many of these behaviors that we repeat have no manifest utility for us, we simply repeat them over and over again because we have become accustomed to them. As they are already established in our behaviors we do not have to make any effort, because they are already consolidated as habits that we execute automatically, in such a way that we can even be thinking about something else at the same time that we do them.

All this set of behaviors to which we get used to is the fruit, the consequence, of our mental contents, of the mental movement that exists previously and that is leading us according to the thoughts that in every moment are in that space.

In many occasions we feel obliged to act in a certain way because there exist in our space of consciousness a series of thoughts that have much strength, much consistency, in such a way that they have the capacity to decide for us, to mark the direction in which we must act and we only limit ourselves to obey without thinking too much about the consequences that may have to act in a certain way in a concrete moment.

If we understand that this happens to us frequently, we can take measures to not act in such a mechanical, automatic way. Just by being aware that this mechanism works this way, our way of coping with it can change, in the sense that we can slow down this mental movement by not acting as impulsively as we often do.

This can only be achieved if we get used to observe that space of consciousness where those thoughts that try to direct us appear. If we go ahead we will be able to stop that tendency, we will be the ones who will end up making the decisions and not so much that vicious circle that many times is created and that we cannot stop.

Our mind is constantly using a lot of information and it is difficult for that information to appear organized. It is what explains that in many occasions we feel a great confusion inside us, and it is because the information that in that moment is being expressed in that space is confusing, it does not help us to find a solution to the problem that we are having in that instant; it is not useful to solve the difficulty that in that moment we are facing.

If we get used to stop and analyze what we think, with practice it will be much easier for us to make decisions, because in our reason there will be a greater clarity that will help us to organize much better the information that at that moment is there, in that space where some thoughts are joined with others and we draw conclusions and make decisions that many times we execute in a mechanical way, without controlling what we are doing.

March 14, 2020

Our mind works mechanically as long as we allow it, as long as we act unconsciously and let it direct our own thoughts, but it is true that we can intervene in the way it works and vary the course and direction of the contents that at a given moment are occupying our mental space.

Simply by being observers, we will become aware of the thoughts that at any given moment are spreading there, we will be aware that if these thoughts are maintained for a certain time, they end up influencing us in such a way that in the end they force us to carry out a specific action.

Before this happens, before we end up performing a certain behavior, forced by our own mind, we can modify the course of our own thoughts in such a way that we can avoid ending up performing unwanted actions. Because in many occasions we act, but later we regret what we have done, and it is for having acted impulsively, for having allowed ourselves to be guided by what our reason dictated to us at that moment.

This process is like a chain that goes around and around and that at a certain moment we can stop, if we use the appropriate tools and have the precise knowledge about the functioning of this mechanism. Once we learn to stop this chain, this vicious circle, we can reach a certain control over ourselves, over the functioning of our mind. And this will then be reflected on the outside, in the actions we carry out. We will see that we begin to stop acting like a robot directed by an automatic mechanism over which we have little control.

All this is possible if we use the right tools, if we use the observation of ourselves, of our understanding, of our thoughts, of that space where we integrate all those contents coming from our memory that extend to our consciousness and in our inner voice, where all those expressions that appear in our mind are repeated over and over again and that in many occasions alter our state of mind, our vision of things and our way of understanding the world and the life that surrounds us.

March 15, 2020

When we talk to ourselves, through that inner voice where our thoughts are expressed, we realize what is important to us at that moment. At each moment of the day it may vary; the most repeated thoughts may be different, related to different topics. Depending on the situation in which we find ourselves, so are our thoughts.

If we realize that these thoughts have no limitation, they can be repeated over and over again indefinitely; and when they stop repeating themselves, new, different ones arise, related to another subject. Our mind is an inexhaustible source of thoughts that involve us, that make us pay attention to a series of contents that at that moment we believe are important for us. As we pay attention to these contents, we begin to create a structure of thought, a system by which we analyze reality, what happens to us, even what happens to the people with whom we have some kind of relationship in the context in which we live.

Everything is first produced there, in our mind, which is the territory where thoughts are born and where we build our vision of things, of the world around us, and where we make the decisions that later influence the course of our life, our destiny.

That is why our mind is so important. It is the reason why we must investigate a little more, observe ourselves a little more to analyze what we do, to know if it has a sense or a meaning for us. Then we will find out the usefulness of our actions, of our behaviors and of each and every one of the thoughts behind what we do every day.

Then we will learn to use it properly, as an instrument that can benefit us in many moments of confusion and anguish, especially when we feel blocked or when we do not know what to do when faced with a problem or difficulty.

If we observe ourselves we will realize that it has a great utility, that it is not something mechanical that is given to us by nature and that we need in order to survive. We can only see its usefulness if we know how to go a little further, if we stop and observe our behaviors; the causes behind what we constantly repeat. We will realize that some thoughts are repeated more than others, that sometimes vicious circles are established that we cannot stop and that lead us to the constant repetition of the same idea.

March 16, 2020

Our mind is a very valuable instrument that we should try to understand in its totality, because this will be of benefit to our own personal well-being. Everything that is represented there can weaken or strengthen us, depending on its contents.

Therefore, we must act in such a way that we always keep in mind the importance of all those mental processes that take place within us, which have a principle and a reason for being.

It is important, in this sense, to be aware of our internal conversation, of what we say to ourselves in many moments, because if we stop to observe ourselves we can understand many behaviors and habits that we have daily; we can understand many emotional wounds that we have caused ourselves, without being aware.

We only have to look at what is happening inside us, in our inner world. We must pay attention to everything that appears on that screen that is our mind, our consciousness, where thoughts, images, ideas, contents, interests, desires are constantly being published, leading us along a certain path.

We, without knowing it, are giving ourselves to all those kinds of contents that are automatically executed in that space. Therefore, it is important that we make an exercise of attention to observe how these internal movements are produced within us.

Then we will verify what it is that causes us discomfort or suffering. We will become aware of the kind of thoughts we have; which ones are more abundant of the whole set of thoughts that come to our mind throughout the day. We can observe the form we give to many ideas we have; we will understand why many of them fail over time. We will realize how we join some ideas with others to reach surprising, disconcerting conclusions, which lead us to reinforce our own beliefs, many of which turn out to be wrong.

Just by observing all this, we will obtain results. The mere observation is a valid procedure to reduce those useless thoughts that only make us lose valuable time, because in reality they do not lead anywhere, they do not cause any benefit for us.

We must flee as far as possible from this kind of thoughts, closing our consciousness to all those toxic contents that are conditioning us in our decision making.

If we get used to tread this ground, this space of consciousness, we will achieve great achievements, we will make great changes in our life; our decisions will be more solid, more realistic and useful; we will learn to separate the harmful contents from those that make us improve; we will find a meaning to everything that has happened to us so far.

In reality, our life is the consequence of everything that has previously passed through our reason; we are the consequence of our own thoughts. They are thoughts that belong to us, because they are part of us and have arisen in our own consciousness, and from there they have been producing new ones.

They are the cause of our situation. They are the beginning of everything we do; of how we interpret our own life and how we see others when we relate to them.

Everything that is established in our mind provides us with the circumstances in which we end up living. Everything has a beginning and develops right there, in our own consciousness. Mainly for that reason, we have the responsibility to promote in us another way of seeing the world, we must try to stop all those thoughts that produce us some damage.

We have to throw them out of there, because these are the ones that end up altering us in some way, when they take over our will and grab us completely. They are all those thoughts that show themselves over and over again, that belong to us because they are ours, but that are related to negative aspects of the past, to experiences that constantly transport us to previous situations that were negative for us.

We cannot give in to this mechanism that tries to repeat again and again the bad experiences of the past. This mechanism is established in us, in such a way that it influences our judgments, our conclusions and the different interpretations we have of what is happening to us at each moment.

All this remains in our memory, and when we least expect it, it jumps out, emerges again to our consciousness and alters us and influences us in our way of seeing the world at every moment.

March 17, 2020

We have to learn to govern ourselves. In this way we will properly order reality, we will put everything in its place and our suffering will diminish.

It is necessary that we give the importance it deserves to all these formations that are created in our mind, that are within us and that are the ones that ultimately direct and condition us. For this we must not only stay on the surface, we must go a little deeper beyond what we see and what we do.

If we really want to achieve a transformation, we must suppress what is causing us any harm, so we have to learn to observe all those internal movements, all that inner conversation we have with ourselves. It is there where we can guess all those contents; where we can discover all those thoughts that many times block us and dominate us in such a way that negativity multiplies inside us, and all this then affects what we do outside.

We have to be aware that our mind is determining us at every moment. If there are elements in our consciousness that create confusion, our life will be confused; if they dispose us to negativity we will end up being negative; it depends on the attention we pay to those contents.

We have to know that this is where they are born and that they give meaning to everything we do, to everything we think. Subsequently, they compose within us a way of seeing reality, a way of ordering our own ideas. Everything depends on the point of view we adopt when evaluating everything that happens to us; it depends on where we direct our gaze; all subsequent thoughts will be the result of that.

That is why it is important to observe the information we have in our mind, since within that information there is a series of contents that are repeated more frequently, and those are the ones that really have an effect on us in the end, on our way of understanding reality. They may be temporary or transitory thoughts, but they are forcibly established in that space; any movement we make is infused by those kinds of thoughts.

If we feel that there is an alteration within us we must pay attention to the thoughts that are most abundant in our consciousness at that moment, because those are the ones that are really burning us inside, they are the ones that are imposing themselves over other kind of more positive thoughts.

March 18, 2020

In our mind the same thoughts are always repeating themselves. We let ourselves be guided by them, by all those expressions that arise in our conscience loaded with emotions that are pushing us towards a series of actions that are enveloping us and launching us towards a specific direction.

Everything starts in that interval in which some thoughts are transmitted and we allow ourselves to be conquered by them, in such a way that in the end they end up guiding us, channeling us along a certain path.

My recommendation is to observe this process to discover how it works, to see how a series of thoughts spread over our own will, around our mind.

If we dedicate ourselves to pay attention to this mechanism, we can realize how many behaviors that we develop throughout the day originate.

Everything comes from there, there is no secret mystery. Everything is first processed in that space through a series of thoughts that come together, while we get used to them, until in the end we focus on those that are most important and we are unable to separate ourselves from them, so they continue to be exposed again and again there, on that screen that is our consciousness.

If we are aware of these processes and we notice them in due time, we will be able to correct this submission, this submission, that in many occasions we have towards everything that passes through our reason.

If we investigate a little bit all this that happens within us, in our consciousness, we will be able to escape, in some way, from all those vicious circles that in many occasions determine us and from which it is difficult to get out.

If we observe ourselves we will know how they originate, we will arrive at the beginning, we will see how they are formed and how they are established and remain there for long periods of time. In such a way that in the end we get used to them, so they develop even more, if we do not correct it.

The functioning of our mind is based on repetition. There is no concrete order of all the elements that are exposed in it. There are thoughts that last longer in time than others, which seem to evaporate more easily. That to which we pay attention grows and develops even more, compared to those other elements to which we do not give importance.

All these manifestations that take place there, constitute the beginning of what we end up being, of what we end up doing. In the end all this becomes concrete in our own actions, it becomes visible in our behaviors. If there is confusion within us, it will also appear outside, in our actions, in our way of being in the world.

March 19, 2020

When you disconnect a little from reality and no stimulus influences or distracts you, you get to connect with your inner world, with whatever is in your mind at that moment. It is easier for you to observe what is happening on that screen that is your consciousness, which is where the contents that arise in that space from your memory are manifested.

When you disconnect from external influences, your gaze is directed towards your inner world. In this way you can discover many things about yourself, about your own mental mechanism, about all those processes that happen inside and that at every moment are determining you, conditioning you, since everything you do, first originates in that space.

If we pay attention to all those things that happen inside us, in our own interior, we will find many explanations about our behaviors, about our way of thinking, about our ideas and beliefs, about our way of understanding the world. It is just a matter of observing how we associate our thoughts, all those contents that appear in our consciousness.

All this gives rise to our particular way of interpreting the world, of understanding the life in which we live. All of this conditions us, determines us, and indicates the way we behave: the way we act and relate to the people around us.

Therefore it is important that we direct our gaze towards ourselves, towards our inner world and that at least for a few moments we separate ourselves from the external world, from the material world, from all those stimuli that surround us and that in many occasions distract us, in such a way that we allow ourselves to be trapped and in the end we end up diverting ourselves from what we should really do, or from what we would really like to do.

If we pause in time and look at ourselves, we will understand why we are the way we are and why we end up doing the behaviors we do.

Everything arises first of all in our mind; it is where everything starts from. Depending on how the elements are distributed in it, so will be our thoughts, our ideas and our way of interpreting what happens to us at each moment.

We can only understand what happens to us if we stop to observe ourselves, if we analyze our own thoughts: our particular way of thinking. Only in this way we will understand ourselves, we will find the explanations we need to understand what happens to us, or what has happened to us previously in our past experiences.

It is the best way to reach the knowledge of ourselves, of what we really are. Everything is concentrated there, in those contents that arise from our memory and that appear in our mind.

That is why we can observe them, because they come to light in our consciousness; that is where they manifest themselves, and if we pay a little attention we can detect and analyze them.

We will soon realize if they are negative or toxic; or if on the contrary they are beneficial for us. It just depends on us stopping and paying attention to what happens in that space, since that is where what we end up doing later is concentrated.

March 20, 2020

Through our mind rushes an endless number of ideas that sometimes isolate us from reality, since they are confusing and plunge us into a deep abyss that brings us closer to suffering.

When we see everything cloudy in our mind, it is because it harbors many negative thoughts that absorb us, while we, in a passive way, renounce other more positive thoughts, so we let ourselves be absorbed by those contents that arise and repeat themselves, even if they are not very beneficial for us.

All this creates a disorder that is established because somehow we allow it. This disorder, over time, is accentuated to the extent that all these thoughts spread throughout our consciousness.

When the darkness is too great, we try to clarify a little bit all that space, so we try to look for explanations to try to understand the reality, both external and internal.

We remember, in these cases, that we can somehow take the initiative; and, therefore, we try to diminish all that mental noise with a more positive, more conscious attitude, trying to guess and to observe all those contents that are being composed in our consciousness, that are somehow taking over our will.

When we realize this, we are aware that we can direct, control in some way, those thoughts that are showing themselves there and that in many occasions paralyze us and lead us to anguish or worry.

If we try to prevent them from increasing, from developing certain contents, we can protect ourselves, with patience, from the deception of our own mind. If we know how to penetrate into our inner world and we realize where our disturbances, our suffering, begin, we can overcome this mechanism, we can isolate certain contents, remove certain thoughts from our consciousness.

So we will find a relief, a certain well-being. We will appease all that noise, thus moderating our reason, so we will improve our own vision of life, of the world around us, of ourselves.

All this will lead us to a certain inner transformation. Thanks to the modification that we can carry out at a mental level of all those contents that in many occasions are accommodated there, in our mind, in an unconscious and mechanical way.

When we achieve this, we find that there is less internal agitation, that our anxiety disappears and a calmness begins to dwell within us that spreads throughout our body.

This is the only way to suppress all that influence that our mind has over us. It is the only way to appease its influence on our behaviors, on our behaviors.

Therefore, we must pay attention to everything that dwells in that space for a prolonged period of time. We have to be aware that they are contents to which we have given importance, in such a way that in the end they end up appropriating our consciousness, until in the end they force us to think in a certain way, to lean towards specific thoughts.

Everything that we end up doing, in the end keeps a relationship with everything that we think in a constant way. Everything we have in our mind affects us in some way, so it is important to contemplate it, to observe it, to keep a certain distance if possible.

We cannot let ourselves be bewitched by the influence of all these contents, since many of them can lead us to confusion, if we allow it.

We must therefore anticipate everything that can harm us. We cannot allow our intellect to disturb us, to rob us of our peace of mind at every moment. We must look into the depths of ourselves, to realize all these oscillations that are within us. It is a matter of observing ourselves a little.

In this way we will find harmony within our inner world. We will achieve an inner well-being that will be our gateway to that other level of consciousness where confusion does not exist; that other space where thoughts stop projecting themselves constantly. When we take that leap into this other dimension, all that mental clatter disappears.

To distinguish this easily, we only need to observe. We will immediately find the beginning of all our problems, of our confusions. It is then that they will begin to diminish, to sink into the oblivion of our memory.

March 21, 2020

Although intervening in our mind is difficult, we can only achieve it through practice and with a series of tools such as observation, mindfulness, meditation and other techniques that we can discover if we make an effort to try to discover what is happening there in each moment.

When we achieve this, we immediately become aware of everything that is constantly manifesting in that space. We come to understand our behaviors and many experiences we have lived in the past. We will find explanations for many things that have happened to us in the past. We will understand that many things happen to us because we act in a certain way, because the reading we make of what we have in front of us leads us to act in a particular way.

If we stop to analyze briefly what is behind our behaviors, we will see clearly that what we have are thoughts that have to do with a particular issue and that at that moment have spread in our mind. We will come to the conclusion that those thoughts are the ones that have led us to act in a particular way at that moment.

Everything we do depends first on a thought. Therefore, we must pay attention to all those contents that are cultivated there, because those contents are the cause of our behaviors, our actions, our attitudes and the way we relate to others.

If we understand that everything that is established in our reason can come to determine us in some way, then our mind will have importance for us and therefore we will be concerned to observe ourselves more and more frequently to see the kind of thoughts that take place in our consciousness.

All this will lead us to know in more detail the way our intellect proceeds. We will know much better how its mechanism works, how is that system that works in a mechanical way and that tries to determine us, to condition us, to take us in a direction that in many occasions we do not want to go, but we feel obliged to continue in it because the thoughts that are behind have too much force, because they have been established there for a long time because we have put our focus of attention on them for some reason.

If we dig a little further and analyze the reasons why we stop and pay attention to some thoughts more than others, we can get to understand this whole mechanism much better, get a better control over it.

March 22, 2020

Our relationship to context influences the way we pay attention to certain content, to certain issues, but it also influences how important those issues are to us. When they are things that we think are not important, we pass them by, we do not put our focus on them permanently, and therefore our mind does not need to accumulate thoughts related to that subject.

The importance we attach to something may also depend on a thought or a set of thoughts. If I think that an issue is important to me for some reason, I am already giving relevance to that issue and therefore that issue is already important. Immediately my mind will try to look for motives, reasons, to convince me that indeed, that issue is important. When I am totally convinced of its importance, I try to pay attention to it, and that is when a great number of thoughts related to that subject will begin to sprout and establish themselves in that space, which will be like a stream of similar thoughts that will try to relate to each other.

This is how our attention works and the process by which we give importance to certain contents. This is what our mind actually does when it focuses only on a particular class of thoughts and repeats them over and over again until they become so intense that in the end they force us to perform a behavior.

Thoughts, therefore, are the food of our mind, and if we put the focus of attention on a subject, our mental system will be in charge of searching in our memory for contents related to that subject. Then we will see that something to which we have never given too much importance, begins to spread, thus attracting our focus of attention, until it occupies a larger and larger space in our consciousness.

We will realize that, in certain periods of our life, due to our circumstances, there are certain matters that begin to be relevant to us that were previously of little importance. And when some time passes they begin to lose interest because we are no longer in the same situation and our focus of attention is no longer placed there but on other contents that at that moment have more interest for us for some reason.

March 23, 2020

Everything is first manufactured in our mind. When we are inclined to pay attention to a subject it is because in that space there is already a large amount of content related to that subject, and that is what moves us to direct our internal gaze towards those elements.

Many times thoughts are linked because they have to do with something that at that moment is of great interest to us, and that is why we keep coming up with content related to that topic, until there comes a time when we can not turn our attention away from them. Then our mind, at that moment, manages to capture all our attention and it is difficult in this case that we deviate from there, that we direct our gaze to other different contents.

When a structure is created with the same thoughts, with a large number of elements that keep a certain relationship, it is difficult for us to get distracted, to turn our attention away from other kinds of elements.

Somehow our attention is also influenced by the mental objects, by the kind of thoughts that are in our mind at any given moment. If they are significant elements, that in those moments have a great importance for us, they possess a great facility to capture all our attention and to catch us without we are very conscious of this process.

The issues that are important to us at any given moment depend on the situations in which we find ourselves throughout the day; they depend on the circumstances and the context in which we live at any given moment. All this can have a great influence on what we are interested in, which can vary or can consist of the same subject that we can be thinking about practically all day long.

It also influences the type of experiences we have had previously. There are issues that we may be quite interested in because of the experiences we have had related to that particular topic. If they have been positive, it is possible that this subject will continue to interest us in the future, in such a way that when the memory of that experience comes to us, it is easy for us to fix all our attention on it, and from then on a great number of thoughts will begin to multiply and will start to arise in our consciousness related to that experience.

In the same way it can also happen with negative experiences, if they have caused in us a great emotional impact that have left a mark, it is also possible that once the memory of these, also begin to arise images related to these experiences that will also cause our attention to focus there.

Something is important to us when it manages to leave an imprint on our memory. When it has the capacity to impact us in some way. To check whether something is important or not, we only need to pay attention to the time we spend thinking about it.

What interests us most changes over time. Our interests change as we have new experiences. What we are interested in at any given moment is also a function of our needs. Our main focus will always be on what we need most, but it may vary throughout the day or it may be a constant need that lasts for long periods of time.

That which we need starts to become relevant to us and therefore we focus all our attention there, which will enable the creation of new ideas and thoughts related to that need. We will focus all our energy there and we will dedicate time to it because at that moment it is the most important thing for us.

When we solve a need, it ceases to be important and therefore we stop paying attention to it, so our thoughts will change, they will be replaced by others that will begin to capture our attention in the same way as the previous ones.

It is all a matter of priorities and the need we have to solve a certain issue. The mental movement works in this way, it is always focused on what is most important at each moment for us, although it may vary depending on the situations we have in front of us and the circumstances in which we live at any given time.

March 24, 2020

It is up to us to analyze our own thoughts in order not to act in a mechanical way. Surely there will be many elements that escape us, because the field of our mind is very wide; it has no defined dimensions or established limits. But we can pay attention to all those thoughts that are repeated the most, those that for some reason are more significant for us, that stand out more.

We should ask ourselves why there are thoughts that are more important to us, out of all the thoughts we may have throughout the day. Surely they will have to do with matters that at that moment are of more interest to us for some reason, for some need.

There are many thoughts that are significant for us in a given period, but cease to be so after some time has passed. The importance that each thought has depends on the situation and the circumstances in which we find ourselves in each period of our life. There may be thoughts that at this moment just pass by, but later on they can become main contents, very important elements, in such a way that they can endlessly repeat themselves and become very important within our consciousness.

It all depends on the situation we are in, on what we are interested in at any given moment and on the place where we have our focus of attention. As soon as there is a subject that interests us for some reason, then thoughts related to that subject will begin to arise.

Our consciousness will be filled with contents related to that particular subject, and when it ceases to interest us, those contents will be replaced by others that will be related to other subjects. Our mind, in this way, is filled and emptied at the same time of thoughts depending on the subject to which we pay attention.

Our attention, in this sense, varies and changes depending on the needs we have at any given moment. Throughout the day we can have our attention focused on multiple subjects; we do not necessarily always have our attention focused on the same place all the time, although sometimes this can also happen.

We change our attention throughout the day because we often change our situation, our context, and therefore our circumstances also change, even the people we relate to throughout the day are also different. Externally we change context and therefore we have the opportunity to live different situations.

All this makes our mind change its focus of attention on many occasions throughout the day, although in the end there are always thoughts to which we pay more attention, regardless of whether we change situations. One can change context, but if there is something that worries you, you can keep in your mental space a series of thoughts more frequently, even if you live a large number of different situations throughout the day.

March 26, 2020

The way we pair our judgments, our thoughts and reasoning affects us and conditions our lives, determining the way we learn from our experiences, from everything around us. That is why we must explore and be attentive to all the signs that life presents us, because that is where our way of understanding the world, each situation, begins.

All this influences and has great consequences on us, since it determines our development, our evolution and our own actions.

Therefore, our way of learning from reality is important, because it influences the type of answers we give later to each and every one of the difficulties that life presents us with.

Our mind never remains still; it is like a constant machine that has an effect on us. It is just a matter of observing and not letting it manipulate us, influence us and determine our responses, our behaviors.

We have to be attentive to each and every one of those thoughts that come into our consciousness. If they are negative, we must turn away; if they are positive, we must take care to reinforce them so that they are repeated more times. If we are attentive, we have the opportunity to do so, we have the opportunity to notice when our mind tries to condition us, to force us to act in a certain direction.

We must learn to control ourselves a little more, to not let ourselves be manipulated by our own mental mechanism, which on many occasions tries to determine us, to lead us in a specific direction.

We have to be aware that this mechanism is very fast and has a great effect on us, on what we do, on our behaviors. They are processes that are executed mechanically, depending on the importance we give to certain contents. We cannot abandon ourselves to what it decides at any given moment. We cannot depend all the time on this mechanism, because we have the capacity to control it, to achieve that it does not have so much effect on us.

We only have to resort to our internal perception to become aware of the mental programs that we are reinforcing without realizing it, without being very conscious of it. We will clearly observe a great number of elements that originate within us and that contain a great amount of information that in some way condition our life.

March 27, 2020

It should be a constant challenge to practice observing ourselves. If we get used to perform this exercise we would become aware of our mental state, of the movement that takes place there of thoughts, images and emotions that usually tends to be a disorganized movement.

The only way to put some order in that space is by paying attention to what happens there, to what happens in our consciousness at certain moments. We would learn much more about ourselves, about our way of thinking, by being aware of all those thoughts that are reproduced in our mind.

We would realize that all that movement that takes place in that space is constant and repetitive. Our mind does not stop feeding itself with contents that are executed over and over again coming from our memory. They are stamped unless we start paying attention to other kinds of different thoughts; then our reason will give a turn to those contents and will start looking for other kinds of different elements to start establishing themselves in that space instead of the ones that already exist.

Our mind will change some thoughts for others depending on the focus of attention we use in each moment. It can vary easily and very quickly from one thought to another, even if they are very different from each other. It is a movement that occurs very quickly and we barely have time to establish some control over this process. That is why most of the time we let ourselves be carried away by this mechanism, which is an automatic system that we all have by nature and is difficult to control.

But if we get to have some knowledge about how the procedure works, we can take certain actions to achieve some control over what we think. We can vary, for example, our focus of attention by de-emphasizing different kinds of thoughts. Then we will see that our mind begins to focus on other kinds of content. It is only a matter of changing, through the use of our own will, some thoughts for others.

March 28, 2020

Everything that catches our attention starts to be important for us at that moment, all our senses focus on that matter forgetting everything else. If it is something that shocks us, we can be aware of that subject for long periods of time, without it disappearing from our mind.

Sometimes our mind is focused on a single subject, so that it tries to develop and create thoughts around that subject, repeatedly. It tries to look for similar thoughts and contents and joins them together until it creates a system of related elements that become stronger and stronger and only ends with the passage of time.

If we understand that this is so, we will understand that many times vicious circles are created that extend over time and that are very difficult to change. It is for this reason, it is because of this system, that it is like a program that is created based on repetitions of the same elements and is gaining more and more strength with the passage of time.

If we are victims of this kind of circles that do not stop and always lead to the same place, we must try to get out as soon as possible, at the slightest opportunity we have. We have to try to paralyze this automatic circular movement by trying to divert our attention to another kind of thoughts that will replace the ones that are there at that moment; it is the only way to face this mechanical system that leads us to repeat always the same thoughts.

Everything depends on the place where we put our attention, on the thoughts that occupy our consciousness at every moment, since these are the ones that compose our vision of things, the ones that force us to perform a series of actions that if we repeat them we get used to them and they become habits that we then find it very difficult to stop.

That is why everything that appears on that screen is important. If we get used to the same contents, the direction of our thoughts will not change, it will always remain the same. We must vary that direction when necessary, adding other different thoughts, putting our focus of attention on other matters more beneficial to us that constitute a mental change, a change in the set of thoughts that at that moment are in that space.

When we look at ourselves, at what we are thinking at that moment, it is like going to the beginning of everything, since it is there, inside our mind, where everything we do, everything we think and the reasoning we use to try to understand what is happening around us begins.

It is very easy to find out what we are thinking at every moment, it is only a matter of observing ourselves, of looking inside ourselves, in that screen that is our consciousness where all those thoughts that we have at every moment are represented. Everything is there, what happens is that it appears in a disordered way and that is why in many occasions a great confusion is created in us.

When we do not find an explanation or when we do not understand very well what is manifesting in that space, it is because there is a conflict in the set of thoughts that at that moment are taking place in our consciousness, in such a way that the information that reaches us is confusing, it requires more data so that we can understand it and see clearly what is happening.

It is in our hands to stop and try to clarify those thoughts, to learn to establish a certain order when necessary. It is about being attentive to that information, to those contents that are emerging and that are filling every space of our mind. It is the first step to make changes within ourselves.

March 29, 2020

Our mental work consumes a lot of energy throughout the day, so it is important to take into account the time we spend paying attention to many thoughts that have no use for us. If we pay attention to them they grow, they are like a plant that sprouts quickly unless we do something to prevent it.

It is important, therefore, to take into account how our mind is managed, since we can waste a great deal of energy and valuable time on any idea that in the end is worthless. Many times we find ourselves executing and repeating behaviors, behaviors that lead us nowhere. All these actions have their origin in a set of thoughts that have been previously established there, we have given them importance because they are meaningful to us and in the end they have settled in our consciousness.

In the end what we end up doing is the product of what arises in that space. We must insist on analyzing and taking into account the kind of contents to which we pay attention, since these are the ones that are going to lead us, that are going to cause us to act in a certain direction and to repeat a series of behaviors that in many occasions are of no use to us.

Time is very valuable and we must take advantage of it in that which has a benefit, instead of wasting it in repeated actions that do not lead anywhere. If we stop and look at ourselves, we will realize what we are doing and how useful it can be. In the case that we understand that these actions do not lead anywhere, we can stop at that moment, establish a pause and change direction.

Our mind can be a great ally if we use it well. There are a multitude of contents that can obscure our vision of things, they can stain our conscience in such a way that it prevents us from taking advantage of all the potential we have inside: our best abilities.

We can sink into the abyss if we only focus on and give free rein to toxic thoughts that the only thing they do is incline us to a series of useless behaviors that do not benefit us in any way.

That is why we must be attentive to what has a place in our mind: what we repeat most often. This will allow us to know the direction that our reason is taking in those moments. It is important to know this if we want to establish some changes in our life. It is the only way to eliminate those negative habits that may be harming us.

The mind, in this sense, is also a source of information for us. If we pay attention to all that multitude of thoughts that are always in it, we will find out what kind of contents are being built in our consciousness, what elements are penetrating with more strength and the effect and the consequences that all this will have for us.

Our main purpose should be to exercise control over ourselves, over that mental movement that sometimes incapacitates us to carry out what we really wish to do, or to execute only those actions that are of benefit. It only requires a small effort on our part. It is just a matter of understanding that everything that is shown in that space influences us for better or for worse.

March 30, 2020

If we are attentive and observant we can notice that movement deep within our inner world. Sometimes it is necessary for us to do so, especially when we want to establish control over ourselves, over what we are thinking at any given moment. In this way we can stop our mind from feeding on toxic thoughts.

If in those moments we are not attentive, we can give free rein to our imagination, and in this way our intellect can cultivate a reality that is especially different from the one we observe, from the one that exists outside.

If we do not put a brake on that movement, there are many thoughts that will be prolonged over time in our consciousness. That is why we are required to establish a certain order within ourselves. If we get to know ourselves a little better, we will manage to placate that mental movement that tries to decide for us, that develops conflicts and contradictions in our own consciousness through a series of toxic thoughts that are articulated one after another, creating mental representations that impulsively repeat one after another over time, influencing our own feelings, our emotions.

We can intervene in some way to change the direction of these processes. It is only a matter of working on our attention in that point of our consciousness where our ideas, our reflections and reasoning are woven. It is right there where everything takes place, where everything begins. It is there where the origin of our own actions is.

Nothing is fortuitous, everything is the fruit of what we think in the first place. That is why we must be attentive to the form of our thoughts, to how they are expressed, to the existence of certain negative contents in our mind coming from the past; all this forms a mental garbage that builds our vision of things; they are like a stain on our consciousness.

Everything depends on the attention we pay to a specific kind of contents. From there originate the actions that we then perform: the type of activity that we carry out. Everything is a function of the movement of the mind, of all that variety of thoughts that move in our consciousness.

The fact that one thought follows another is the result of the type of attention we pay to certain contents, to certain stimuli. In this way these elements are established in this space, they give meaning to all those things that we think and that in some way guide us, at the same time that they sometimes cause a certain internal disorder.

We, unintentionally, abuse in many occasions to be focused, to be centered in the same thoughts. Hence our obsessions that often haunt our heads and from which we are unable to detach ourselves.

Somehow we have to use our attention on ourselves to follow those thoughts and analyze in more detail the conclusions we are reaching: the interpretations we are making about that particular situation we have to face.

The thoughts that arise are actually cultivated by us when we pay attention to a particular subject. This causes that on the tapestry of our consciousness begin to emerge elements related to what we are giving importance to at that moment. If it is a subject that causes us disturbance, surely in our mind will appear forms, thoughts that will be grouped and that will cause us disturbance, uneasiness, a feeling that we are facing a difficulty that we do not control at that moment. The rain of thoughts that will appear in this case will have those characteristics, that condition.

March 31, 2020

What happens in the mind determines us, so we must know how to manage it in an increasingly conscious way. For this it is necessary that we observe ourselves more frequently, to see what is produced in that space, because that is where everything begins, where everything that we are starts.

Everything comes from there, from that place where thoughts are constantly generated and repeated over and over again, in such a way that our attention is trapped trying to discover all those contents that extend little by little throughout the length and breadth of our consciousness. Once our attention is fixed, it is then very difficult to divert it to another place, to a different kind of thought or to other mental objects.

When all our attention and energy is focused on a particular kind of thought, we end up performing an action related to the contents that we have in our mind at that moment, so we can say that we are directed by the process or mental movement that at that moment is occurring in that space of our consciousness. Then we act in a mechanical way, without hardly controlling what we are doing, since we only limit ourselves to obey in an unconscious way what our mind is dictating to us.

In reality, most of the time we function in this way, we limit ourselves to repeat what the mental movement that takes place there dictates to us. However, we can moderate it, exercise some control over it if we are first aware that this process works this way.

Once we know how it works, we can try to put a stop, in some way, to all those impulsive actions that many times we have and that we execute again and again without any control. We can only achieve this if we are conscious at every moment of what is happening, of what we are doing or of the thoughts that we have in our consciousness at that moment.

It is easy to realize if we get used to observe ourselves, if we are aware of our reactions and behaviors, of what we say when we speak to others. It is enough for us to be a little observant to realize all those processes that are behind. There is a whole mechanism that works in a mechanical way that makes it possible for us to act in a certain way.

We will realize that it establishes a script that marks the direction we must follow. Only through our will we can make modifications in that script, we can achieve a certain independence with respect to what it is constantly dictating to us. We will feel that we have more freedom when deciding, because our actions will stop being so mechanical and repetitive.

When we have the habit of observing ourselves to discover what is behind everything we do, what we think, we have the opportunity to see results in a short time. When we realize that some habits stop repeating themselves, we begin to have the feeling that we think things a little better before acting, before doing something; then we realize the benefits of self-observation, which helps us to become aware of what we do at all times and the consequences of thinking in a certain way, feeding some thoughts that are not beneficial to us.

All this we can only discover with practice, if we get used to carry out this exercise where we must look at ourselves, stop a little before making a decision. If we get used to act in this way, we will immediately begin to experience great changes in our life; we will have the feeling that we are the ones who govern the mind and our own behaviors.

All this will then be reflected in some aspects of our personality: we will have greater self-confidence; we will make better decisions since we will no longer act as impulsively as we did before; we will learn to analyze things a little better when we have to decide on important issues; we will reach a greater serenity that will then be reflected in our dealings with others, in our relationships with those people who surround us in our immediate context. It will have multiple benefits to reach a certain control over what we do, over many negative thoughts that have the habit of repeating themselves over and over again.

4. Awareness

April 1, 2020

Our transformation begins when we become aware of what is happening, when we become conscious of our habits, which have been established over time and which have gradually shaped our circumstances.

When we try to make changes in our lives and strive to prevent some of our behaviors from repeating themselves, then we become aware of the consequences for us of acting in a certain way, of living under a mentality that inclines us to think in the wrong way.

When we reach this point we see that many of our reasonings have not been correct, possibly because we have made a mistake when we have made a reading of what has been happening to us previously.

And the fact is that everything depends on the information that we have already stored and that we have acquired throughout our past experiences. Depending on how we use the information we already have, we will be able to solve our difficulties and all those problems that arise later.

If all those contents already stored in our memory are not well articulated, if we do not give them a structure that has a certain logic and usefulness, they may not be very useful when we need them.

That is why it is important that we have the habit of analyzing the circumstances that surround us, our situation, when making decisions that may affect us in the future.

We are used to act impulsively, without thinking about the consequences of our behavior. Even to many of our habits we do not give them too much importance, so that we repeat them over and over again without realizing that with this we are establishing a way of life that if it is not beneficial then we will suffer the consequences and we will realize over time that this kind of behavior was not the most advisable.

April 2, 2020

We get used to always think about the same thing, we do not try to forge in our mind another kind of thoughts that crystallize in new actions. We get used to the same habits that we repeat over and over again, without realizing the consequences that this can have for us.

Our mind is like a machine that always works in the same way; its main function is to retrieve thoughts from memory and introduce them into our consciousness. From there, these thoughts are concentrated, joining one with the other, and give rise to our actions, which we repeat over and over again thanks to this mental movement that makes the same thoughts always remain.

It is like an automatic mechanism that never stops and that makes us function many times in the same way. We do it because we get used to this system and we do not measure the consequences that this has. It is a mechanism that belongs to our own nature and it is difficult to control: to make it work in a very different way.

It is difficult to manipulate. It is difficult to make it work in a different way. Although it is true that if we know how it works, it can be quite useful for us to be able to make some modifications, some changes within ourselves.

We can become aware of this functioning, of the thoughts that we have in each moment and from there we can work in some way to try to suspend, as far as possible, certain thoughts; contents that we understand that are not beneficial for us. If we try to do this something will change: our attention will focus on other kinds of thoughts and we will see that we will begin to function in a different way. This will be clearly seen in the kind of behaviors we engage in.

The way to get there is difficult. It is a matter of doing this practice frequently so that we will see significant changes. Simply by observing, we will see that some thoughts stop repeating themselves. When these take shape and begin to become stronger is when we act in an automatic way, without being aware that we are focused on the same thoughts; but when we observe those elements that try to dominate us, they lose their strength and their influence on us.

In the end it is a matter of our intellect not determining us. We cannot allow ourselves to be under the tutelage of this automatic mechanism that influences us in such a way that it is carving our own destiny without us being able to do anything to avoid it.

Most of our problems are caused by the way we

function on a mental level, by the movement of our own mind and above all by the thoughts to which we pay the most attention; that is where our greatest difficulties and problems come from. Everything is a function of how we use our reason to make decisions and solve the various difficulties that we face throughout our lives.

A mind that does not work properly allows all those problems to accumulate, until it reaches a point where it is very difficult to turn back and try to find a solution. That is why we must be willing to make changes in the way we function internally. We cannot allow a wall full of difficulties to be built inside us, built by ourselves without us being aware of it.

April 3, 2020

We are always accompanied by our mind, that is why it is so important. When we are alone it always accompanies us, it shares with us thoughts, images, ideas that distract us, that make us forget at that moment that we are alone. It always goes with us, wherever we go; it always accompanies us and provides us with thoughts to fix our attention on.

It always provides us with contents that are being transformed and producing new contents, in such a way that it is a mechanism that never stops. It is always producing ideas, many of which are repetitive and many others are not very useful, because it needs to generate all these contents in order to expend energy.

The mind does not have time to stop and reflect on whether certain thoughts are positive or negative, whether they are useful or not for us at that moment.

It only limits itself to produce a set of contents related to some subject that at that moment are of interest to us, and from there it joins some elements with others, establishing a direction in which the successive thoughts that arise in our consciousness from that moment on will pass.

If we understand that this is a mechanical, automatic mechanism, there is hardly any freedom left for us to decide about it. We have, in this sense, little room to take control of this system, which is characterized by a repetitive activity in which we can hardly intervene if we are not aware of its functioning.

It is a complex system that has a life of its own, that works without us being aware of its functioning, of what is happening in that space, in such a way that it itself is in charge of organizing its contents, of establishing a structure and a direction in thought.

Only when we are conscious is when we can reach a certain control over it; we can prevent, in this sense, that it determines us, that it is the one that marks the direction of those thoughts that then end up being transformed into actions of so much repetition in our consciousness.

April 4, 2020

We can interrupt this flow of contents that takes place in our mind if we are aware of the thoughts that at that moment are being reproduced in it. It is a good way, an interesting exercise, so that certain ideas stop reproducing automatically in our consciousness.

This is important because if we remain hooked to certain thoughts, which are leading us down a path that we do not want, in the end we end up performing repetitive actions that have no benefit for us.

But stopping this process is not so simple, because it is part of an automatic mechanism that orders thoughts as it sees fit: sometimes it orders them in one way and other times in another. It does not have a logic that always repeats itself in the same way. This is what leads us to confusion on many occasions, it is what makes us think one thing and the opposite in very short periods of time.

If we manage to make some changes it will always be an achievement for us, because many negative thoughts will disappear. We must stop feeding our own mind with junk content that does not lead us anywhere, only to waste time on things that have no use.

We must get used, therefore, to pay attention to all those elements that are expressed there, that are shaping a particular way of thinking that in the end is what will mark our own decisions, the direction we take in life.

There are some thoughts that are the most repeated and therein lies the key to everything. The thoughts that mark the direction to follow are those that are repeated more frequently in that space, those are the ones that point the way.

In this sense it can be easy for us to detect them, it is just a matter of noticing what we think most of the time, throughout the day, what kind of expressions are the most constant, what ideas we repeat most often. That is the key to everything, it is what occupies our greatest mental activity, so it is what determines us in the end.

Once we locate that set of thoughts that have found

a refuge there and that our consciousness collects to give them importance, we can stop to find out if that kind of content is beneficial or not for us. In the case that those elements are negative we should try to change our approach, putting our focus on other kind of thoughts more useful and healthy.

April 5, 2020

We need to reach a greater clarity in our consciousness, to know how to detect, above all, those moments of internal conflict, those moments of blockage in which we are the ones who build our own difficulties.

We must learn to be aware to know how our mind works, to see how some thoughts are joined with others, so that in the end we end up building an interpretation of reality according to those thoughts that have previously settled in our consciousness.

All this then has an effect on the way we see the world, on the way we see reality. Everything that happens previously there, then conditions us in all the things we do. That is why it is necessary that we observe all that succession of thoughts that form our vision of reality.

We will realize that there are some thoughts that are more common than others that are repeated more frequently, and also that there are certain elements, mental contents, that sometimes distort reality, since they form a series of mistaken beliefs about what we live.

Faced with this, we must know at all times what our position is. We must get used to being above this mechanism. We have to learn to reject all those ideas and thoughts that try to keep us away from reality, from the world around us. We must also learn to detect those contents that create emotional wounds: all those elements that have to do with memories of the past, with traumatic experiences that we did not overcome in the past and that come back again and again to our mind, in the form of memories.

April 6, 2020

Our mind is an automatic mechanism, but we have the faculty to reach a certain control over it. With a little practice and willpower on our part, we can observe the thoughts that are repeated the most, those that are reproduced over and over again in that space. We can break this movement, this vicious circle, if we focus on other kinds of thoughts, other ideas and other issues.

We have the capacity to be able to decide what we think, although a large part of our mental mechanism is an automatic, unconscious mechanism. We can examine in detail what is being produced at each instant there and at the same time we can eliminate those thoughts if we focus on other thoughts, if we direct our attention to another subject where there will be other kinds of elements: other thoughts different from the ones we have in our consciousness at that moment.

I believe that knowing this is important because we waste a lot of time leaving our mind to its free will, allowing it to manipulate us and to reason for us, without counting on our will. We allow it for long periods of time to take charge of everything, to make decisions for us. And the fact is that most of the time we allow everything that manifests itself in that space to dominate us: to impose on us a certain way of seeing things. We cannot allow this unconscious mechanism that we all have inside us to dispose us to act in an automatic way, as if we were a remote-controlled robot.

We can try to avoid it if we are aware of what is represented there. It is of vital importance the attention, the place where we put the focus of attention. Everything starts from there: the thoughts that will arise and the actions that we will later carry out as a result of those thoughts.

If we are present at all times, if we are aware of ourselves, of everything that happens around us and within our inner world, we can do extraordinary things, such as controlling, to a certain extent, what we think. We can put a certain order in our own mental mechanism, and this will be beneficial for us, no matter how little order we achieve.

This operation is not so simple. Since we are accustomed to function in a mechanical, unconscious way. It is difficult to achieve success in this area, but more and more people are achieving a certain mastery over themselves thanks to meditation and other techniques. This can be clearly seen in the change of habits that some people achieve through the use of their own will, striving every day to try to dominate themselves to achieve to be above their own thoughts, what their mind asks them to do.

April 7, 2020

Everything that appears in our mind does it in a disorganized way. Groups of contents are created and from there they try to mark a direction in our thought; it is what marks the idea that we have next, and so on.

They are elements that arise in a mechanical way, and therefore it is a process that is difficult to control. It is almost impossible to try to organize the contents in real time, at the same time as they are being produced.

What we can do is to try to be aware, observing what is manifested there, because if they are negative contents or that can cause us some harm, we can try to change our focus of attention to other elements and other issues that may be more beneficial to our mental and emotional health.

This exercise of awareness can only be acquired through practice, through the continuous observation of what we think. As we practice it we will see some results and with time it will be easier to exercise some control over this mechanism that we all have inside and that by nature works in a mechanical way.

We must make this effort to be conscious because everything that moves in there, in our mind, in the end influences us in one way or another. If we are not conscious it ends up determining us, because our behaviors will be conditioned by what is produced there. We cannot always act under the orders of a mechanism that works in an automatic way and that we hardly control.

That is why we must make use of our will, to try to be a little freer, to decide for ourselves, having the feeling that we are the ones who have the reins of our life, of what is established in that space.

We will feel better with ourselves, since we will control that which conditions us, that which makes us live in confusion many times, that creates imaginary conflicts and problems and difficulties where in reality they do not exist.

We must get used to take control, modifying what is necessary to try to direct our thoughts, so that they go in the right direction, in the direction in which we really want to go. Then there will be in us a coherence between what we think and what we end up doing. This will be reflected in our behaviors, in our attitude, in our way of being in the world and with others. Everything that happens in our mind has an effect, a reflection on the outside, in the way we behave and in our actions.

It is only a matter of making this effort to be more and more conscious of what we do, of what we think, of the contents that we cultivate and to which we pay more attention, because these are the ones that will have an effect on us, they are the ones that create a mental structure that guides us in every moment, the one that makes the decisions and marks the direction in which we should go.

As we practice this exercise of consciousness to try to reach a certain control over our mind, we will begin to see results. We will feel better about ourselves, since we will no longer live so conditioned by this powerful force, which is a mechanism that never stops, that tries to dominate us every time it has a chance.

Once we get to control our mind somewhat, we will see that most of the contents that manifest there are more positive for us, more beneficial. In reality, the mental garbage, all those negative and toxic contents that often arise, only appears when we let it function without control; then it fills with undesirable contents.

If we gain control of this space, we will achieve greater harmony: our thoughts will begin to follow the line of what we really want to be, what we want to do. We will feel that there is a greater coherence between our thoughts and what we really are.

April 8, 2020

In our mind great changes take place from one moment to another, suddenly, in such a way that we hardly have time to have a control over them. When we want to realize it, a set of thoughts appears that takes hold of us, of our attention, and we barely have margin to be able to stop this movement that begins to mark the direction in which we should direct our actions.

Everything happens very quickly and without us realizing it. When we begin to be conscious, we realize that we are doing something simply because it is a repetitive action, when we turn a behavior into a habit by force of repeating it, when we reinforce in this way a mental program that we are developing over time by acting in a mechanical and unconscious way.

This is why it is so difficult to achieve control over it, because it is a mechanism that works in an automatic way, in which there are very sudden changes that are executed very quickly, depending on the impact that a particular thought manages to have on us. If at a specific moment a very significant content arises that is related to a past experience that has had an impact on us, then it will capture our attention very quickly and all our energy will be focused on maintaining that mental content as long as possible.

This is how our mind works and that is why we must take into account the great influence that all these processes have on us. If we know their influence and their effects we can act in time, before they occur; we can take some measures to not end up acting in such a mechanical way. If we dedicate a short space of our time to know what is happening, we will start to see results very quickly.

April 9, 2020

Mental objects once they become established and gain strength, are difficult to remove. They tend to repeat themselves and become associated with others like them. And if they are very important to us they grow in the space of our consciousness, in such a way that they become more and more widespread until they manage to capture all our interest. Then it is when we begin to pay attention to those concrete contents, leaving aside other elements that at that moment are no longer important to us.

If we do a little research we can get to know the reasons why certain contents gain importance to the detriment of others. We can find out what may be behind our interests, but first we need to get to know ourselves well. Then we will know why we react in a certain way to a situation; we can intuit what may be behind our behaviors, what it is that moves us to go in a particular direction and not in another.

If we know ourselves we will find many explanations about our way of acting, about our personality and about everything that is behind and what has caused us to live in specific circumstances. If we have this curiosity we can find explanations to many situations that we have lived and for which at the time we did not find any answer to help us discover the reasons that led us to that situation.

If we have this curiosity we will be able to understand much better our past, the way we reacted to certain significant events. If we have a certain interest in finding out what is behind all those mental processes and movements, we will find many answers that we once needed to understand what was happening to us at that moment. We will come to understand ourselves much better; we will find the causes behind what we are, what has made us the way we are.

Our personality, our psychology and our way of being are nothing more than the result of a mental structure, of a structure of thought that we have been creating in our mind, almost without realizing it, by paying special attention to certain contents that have been important to us for some reason, for some motive.

If we go a little further, we can even find out the reasons why we have felt special interest in certain matters and not in others. We will always find an explanation that will clarify the causes that led us to act in a certain way in the past. Everything is there, everything is in our memory. We only need to rescue it, to order this information in a conscious way and then we will find the answers we need to truly know ourselves, to get to the bottom of things; to the causes of everything that has happened to us and that depended on us, on our will, on our behaviors.

April 10, 2020

Problems are within ourselves, they take shape as we think about them: as we pay attention to them.

When a problem becomes the object of our attention, we get used to think about it, to think about it a lot, to the point that sometimes it is more difficult to fall asleep because of the time we dedicate to focus solely and exclusively on that issue.

In these cases everything that is represented in our mind has to do with that particular problem, all the thoughts that come to our consciousness are related to that issue. That is why it is very difficult to stop thinking about it, once it is established in our mind.

It is as if that space begins to fill with stones that later we have to remove one by one to clear the ground and begin to see things from another perspective, with more clarity. With each thought we place a stone that we must later remove to clear the way for other more constructive thoughts.

When difficulties arise and we do not find a way out, we try to look for explanations that help us to find a solution to get out of that problem, but it does not always appear immediately. Sometimes solutions are delayed, because it is not so easy to find them the first time. It is necessary to have, in these cases, a little patience and tranquility, to trust that sooner or later an answer will be found for that problem.

Having this attitude in the face of difficulties can only be achieved if one really gets to know oneself. If one knows oneself, one can also have a certain knowledge of one's mental system, of how this mechanism works, which is capable of creating difficulties and at the same time solving them.

Within us are the problems and also the solutions to most of the difficulties that life presents us with. It is only a matter of knowing ourselves a little, of knowing how we work inside, of knowing the influence that many mental contents have. This knowledge is what leads us to the conviction that the solutions are also within us. We just have to dig a little because they are there, hidden, waiting for us to discover them.

April 12, 2020

Our mind is a machine that we often misuse, because it is a complicated mechanism and it is difficult to achieve a certain control over it. Only those who have the curiosity to know a little more about how it works, can achieve truly significant changes at the mental level.

To do this, they take care to observe what they think at certain times and analyze the possible consequences that these thoughts may have in the future. They anticipate a little of what may happen if they follow the direction of some mental contents.

If they practice this exercise, they can reach a certain control over the mental movement, over the processes that occur there, in that space of great activity where thoughts and images accumulate in a constant way and with hardly any control.

Those who reach a certain control over their own mind, verify the usefulness that this can have in moments of need: when we have conflicts or it is difficult to solve a difficult situation or a problem. If they master this tool that is their mind, they acquire a very powerful weapon to face each and every one of the problems that we encounter along the way throughout life.

For this reason it is important that we reach a certain knowledge of our mental functioning, of this mechanism that directs us most of the time and to which we obey without realizing many times of the consequences that can have for us to follow the direction that marks us.

There are people who are focused on knowing themselves, who give great importance to their inner world and are constantly looking for explanations because they feel a great curiosity about these issues. In the end, thanks to practice, they manage to progress in their own self-knowledge and then this can be perceived in the attitude they have towards life, in their way of being in the world and in the way they relate to others.

All this curiosity leads them to acquire a great deal of knowledge about themselves, about their mental functioning and about the way in which their thoughts are presented. They have knowledge of the thoughts that are most repeated in their mind, of the reasons why this occurs and of the consequences of focusing on certain contents. They know all this in detail because they carry out the exercise of observing themselves frequently. They are people who observe themselves and others a lot, so they have a fairly deep knowledge of human behavior and all the psychology behind what we do.

In fact, this kind of knowledge is the most important, because it has to do with what we are, with what we do and with the causes behind each and every one of our circumstances, the situations we live. And the fact is that what we end up being is the fruit of our own psychology, of our mental functioning. We are at all times the expression of everything we think at every moment. We are the consequence of the whole set of thoughts that we have had throughout our life. The way they have been organized in our mind is what has been causing our destiny.

Therefore, there is nothing fixed in us, since our thoughts can vary, we can give a twist if we want to our own mentality, our way of thinking and the mental structure we have at every moment. Because in some way we can also intervene in that mechanism; we can change its functioning if we feel that curiosity to observe it, to learn from it.

We can reach a certain control over our thoughts and therefore over our way of living, over our habits, which are the consequence of all those thoughts that we constantly repeat.

In us lies the ability to make changes in our inner world, which will then be reflected and have their effect outside of us, in the world around us, in our relationships and in our way of understanding life and understanding ourselves. Everything that originates in our mind then has a consequence on the outside, in one way or another.

We can intervene in all these processes at an internal level if we are curious enough to go deep inside ourselves to discover what is behind them, to find out what is happening to make us act in a certain way, to make our personality the way it is. All this we can find out if we have the intention to go beyond, beyond what we see outside, beyond what our reason dictates us in every moment, beyond our thoughts. If we go a little deeper we will discover it; we will learn more of this mechanism that is our mind, our human mind.

April 13, 2020

If we know how to take advantage of our mind, to benefit from the good that is in it, we will come to understand ourselves much better, because we will easily find the explanations we need, the causes behind everything that has happened to us, the reasons for our suffering and our conflicts, many of them created by ourselves when we make a wrong reading of reality that leads us to have a confused vision of the things that happen to us.

It is just a matter of getting to know ourselves a little better. And something that we must know is our own mind, its functioning, its mechanism and many of those processes that occur there and that in many occasions condition us, since they determine what we end up doing.

For this we need to be more in contact with that dimension that is our inner world: the world where our thoughts, our emotions and each of the images that arise from memory are spread. If we get used to being in contact with this inner space, we will find many answers to many questions.

That information can only be found there, in the depths of our inner world. We only need to have a certain interest to investigate a little further; then we will discover a whole hidden world, where we can find valuable information about ourselves, about our personality and our conflicts.

All those people who have this curiosity to know themselves a little better every day, to know how they work inside, acquire knowledge and wisdom that cannot be acquired on the outside, because the information they get is only found in their inner world, in themselves and not in other people or in a book they can read. The greatest knowledge you can get to have about yourself is inside you, you just have to be curious enough to discover it.

April 15, 2020

In our mind there is a great variety of elements, so it is difficult to analyze them. These elements manifest for a short period of time and then are exchanged for others. All of them, in one way or another, have an effect on us, on our emotions and moods, on what we end up doing, on our behaviors.

When one of these elements manages to capture a large part of our attention, then it begins to spread throughout our mind and gradually gains more and more strength, until it manages to catch us completely. Thus, when a set of thoughts totally seizes our attention, it gets us to act in a certain direction, it tries to drag us along completely. In the end our actions are conditioned by that kind of thoughts that manage to occupy all the space of our consciousness.

We are not aware of the effects that thoughts have on us, especially those that take total control of our mind. If they are beneficial for us we have nothing to worry about, the problem comes when they are negative contents. Then we feel a sense of blockage, that we cannot move forward or even that we are going backwards. Many of these contents impede our development, influence our emotions and our moods. These negative thoughts are the basis of our suffering.

We have to give the importance it deserves to our mind, because in it can extend elements that can make us function in a negative way for us. And all this can be due to the kind of contents that at that moment have settled there because we have given them importance or we have paid too much attention to them.

We are not aware of the importance that this has for the course of our life, because this is what causes us to have bad habits and over time we find it very difficult to reverse them, to try to eliminate them.

It is important, therefore, that we know this procedure that our mind uses from which it can introduce in that space that is our consciousness, a series of contents in the form of thoughts that can be harmful to us. It can do it because in those moments we are not conscious neither of those thoughts nor of the consequences that they can have for us in the future. In that instant it is our mind that is in control and it is the one that organizes the contents without us hardly intervening. We simply limit ourselves to follow its instructions, without going any further.

As we become more and more conscious and our information about how we function inside is increasing, we gradually manage to avoid having so much influence on us, because we realize the effects of a negative way of thinking or mental content.

Every time we observe ourselves we acquire more information about ourselves, about what is harmful to us and what is beneficial. For this reason it is advisable that we get to know ourselves better and better, to know that a thought can have consequences that we can then see clearly in our daily life, in what we do or in the way we relate to those around us. Each thought can provoke in us a reaction, an emotion, a mood or a behavior that if we repeat it many times can become a bad habit if that initial thought is not beneficial for us.

For this reason it is important that we know how our mind works, of all those mental processes that take place within our internal world that influence our way of understanding the world, in our way of reasoning and drawing conclusions about all those things that happen to us throughout the day.

We will realize that most of the time we live determined by our mental system, by the movement of our mind and by all those processes that are always with us, wherever we go. But at the same time that we realize this, we will also be aware that we can intervene, that we can introduce some important changes in this mechanism so that it does not work so mechanically, so automatically. We can make use of a series of tools such as observation or meditation that can help us to diminish the effects that the mind has on us.

April 16, 2020

It is easy to realize the tendency of our thoughts, especially when we observe what we do throughout the day, since our actions are the fruit of what we constantly think. If we are aware of our behaviors we will know at all times the kind of thoughts that are going through our head, because those are the ones that are setting the direction we are following.

It is therefore easy to find out at all times the kind

of contents that are in our mind. It is interesting to know this, especially when we need to establish a change of habit. We must keep in mind that at that moment we have to change our mentality, that we have to develop another kind of thoughts and change our focus towards another kind of contents that are more beneficial for us, because those will be the ones that will spread in our mind and the ones that will force us to act in a certain way.

When we intend to establish a change of habits it is also important that we make an effort to change our own routines, all those small actions that we carry out throughout the day and that form the habit we want to suppress. We must make an effort both behaviorally and mentally; then it will be easier for us to make that change that at times we need to change course a little, to change direction.

Undoubtedly our mind can become a great ally if we use it conveniently. For it is important that we have a certain knowledge of its operation, of the processes that take place inside that space where the mental movement takes place. If we have a certain curiosity to know its mechanism we will have a great advantage at the time of establishing changes that can benefit us.

Its knowledge can also help us to transform ourselves, to know how to face suffering, the problems that we often create for ourselves. It can be a great ally if we manage to reach a certain control over it. If we achieve it, it will stop having so much influence over us, it will no longer condition us in the way it usually does.

5. Control

April 17, 2020

Although we have certain tools, we do not feel the need to change a way of thinking, as long as it does not cause us excessive suffering; then we do try to observe ourselves, because we have the need to put an end to that particular mental structure that is making us suffer so much. Then we feel the obligation to solve our problems or the difficulty we are going through at that moment. But if there is no excessive anxiety, no excessive suffering, we let those thoughts that have been written in our consciousness and that have taken over our mind, by repeating themselves, become part of our life, of our daily tasks, of our actions and of our way of understanding the world.

We are not worried that this set of thoughts goes in a certain direction, since in some way it does not seem to cause us any problems. We only try to suspend them, to change them, when we see that we do not have stability, that something is shaky or that we do not find the necessary balance so that everything goes more or less well. If we have the feeling that there is a conflict, then we find like a certain capacity to observe ourselves and to try to put some solution.

April 18, 2020

Our life is the result of all those processes that have taken place in our mind. The contents that have been established there are the ones that have caused us to act in one direction or another. What we have done has been the fruit of what we have previously thought. We are the consequence of all the readings we have made of all those experiences we have lived.

Everything has its origin in our mind and what we end up being is the result of everything we have thought before carrying out an action. It is the one that has been marking our path, every direction we have taken. All decisions are previously taken there and are later transformed into behaviors and actions that we carry out outside, in the context in which we live.

When we repeat certain actions constantly over time, they become habits, which are the ones that mark our destiny and our circumstances at all times. But everything starts in the first place from our mind, from the contents that are established there. That is why this space is of vital importance for us, because it is the starting point for everything we are, everything we do throughout our lives.

It is an instrument that will show us the way at every moment. Sometimes we follow its guidelines without being very conscious of what we do, without going further, without thinking about the consequences of acting in a certain way. In many occasions we do not think about the result of a specific action, we only execute it because we receive that order.

Most of the time we act in this way, we are not

aware of what we are doing. We just repeat over and over again the same behaviors, until we turn them into habits that are very difficult to eliminate. This is how mental movement works, that movement that gradually builds our vision of reality, of everything that surrounds us.

It is difficult to moderate, so we hardly stop to examine ourselves to know a little better all these processes that we have internally and that are very important because they have a great effect on us, on our way of living life and on the rest of the things we do.

All this has to lead us to give the importance it deserves to this instrument that is our mind, because we depend on it twenty-four hours a day and we cannot live apart from what happens there, since in that space there are the necessary processes for us to survive. We need it to be able to cover all our needs and to solve the different difficulties that we face throughout our lives.

For all these reasons it is important and we must be aware of the need to know better how it works, its processes and that mechanism that works tirelessly and that produces one thought after another repeatedly.

April 20, 2020

Everything in our mind is triggered with great ease. It is a mechanism that never weakens, it retrieves contents from memory according to the preference at that moment and makes our understanding go in a certain direction.

The information rescued from the memory is the food of our mind. All those experiences that we have had in the past are represented again in our consciousness, so that we extract from it the information that we need at any given moment. That information subsequently has an effect on our way of understanding the world, of observing the situation we are in.

Everything comes from the information that we have in our mind in each occasion. When we find ourselves in some difficulty it is because at that moment we are confused because we do not find the right information to solve that problem. We try to look for it but it does not appear, although our mind is a movement that does not stop, that constantly tries to look for information that we have stored.

We can be for long periods of time absorbed by a particular problem. We can spend a long time without finding a way out or an alternative to that problem. The information that during all that time is spread over that space does not help us to find a way out. In these cases our mind is not able to find the solution by itself, in an automatic way, as it does in many occasions. It needs to count a little more on our participation.

This means that in these cases it is required that we make an effort to try to reflect and analyze in a more careful way the difficulty we are trying to solve. In these cases we must go a little further, we have to investigate more carefully the causes that may be causing the problem we are having trouble solving. In these cases our capacity for analysis and reflection plays an important role. We must find enough calm to have a space to focus a little more on what at that moment is causing us that inner turmoil.

And it is that our mind cannot always solve all the

difficulties, all the problems that we are going through. It can help us to look for information, to reason and understand the contents that at that moment we have in our consciousness, but it cannot always solve the difficulties in a mechanical and automatic way. There are times when a detailed analysis of reality is required, of the situation in which we are living at that moment. Sometimes we need more information, we cannot limit ourselves to the information we have stored. In other cases, we are required to look for new information that we do not have.

In these cases we are obliged to create that new information to solve that particular problem, since we cannot solve it with the information we already have. In many occasions we do not come up with the alternatives that our understanding proposes us to solve some difficulties. We must try new solutions, through trial and error, until we find the one that solves our situation.

We cannot afford the luxury of waiting for our mind alone to take charge of solving the difficulties that drag on over time, the problems to which we cannot find a solution. In these cases it is required that we make an exercise of will on our part to try to force a way out, a solution when we find ourselves in a problematic situation that is difficult to solve, or in which we remain for long periods of time without being able to find a definitive outcome.

In these cases our intellect is a good instrument that can help us to find the solutions we need. It is a good tool to change our situation in case of need. We can make it work for us, searching for information in our memory so that we can reason more effectively and draw conclusions that will help us find the solutions we need.

Our mind can be a great ally when we need it. If we allow it to lead us by the current that it establishes, then it can be our enemy; but if we use it properly we have an essential tool to face any difficulty, any problem we have in life. We simply must learn to use it to our advantage.

April 21, 2020

Any thought, no matter how small, can provoke an important disorder in our mind, it can make us hesitate, see an obstacle where there is none. If we are aware that this is so, we can cut it in some way, not allowing it to gain strength, not paying too much attention to it.

But we can only achieve this if we know how to explore with astuteness what it is that really diverts us from our true path; if we know how to make an analysis in time, of all those contents that come from that warehouse -which is our memory- and we see how they advance, how they make their way into our consciousness, many times outside our own will.

We will be able to design a more objective way of thinking, more adapted to what we really are. We will realize that there is a greater clarity, a greater radiance in our ideas, in our ways of thinking.

But sometimes it is difficult to explore in all that volume of content that accumulates in that space. It is difficult in these cases to distinguish the true from the false, the real from the unreal. In those moments we are slaves, in a way, of everything that arises there, since it ends up dominating us, because in the end we succumb to its influence.

We have to be aware of this adversity, for it is part of our very nature. That is why we must give greater importance to all those elements that lodge in our mind and that little by little occupy a certain position in our consciousness. We have to be aware, at all times, of that which causes disorder within us.

We must not let ourselves be deceived by what we think at a given moment, because this can take over our will and can force us to perform a series of actions with which we will not agree later.

If we allow all these contents to oppress us, we can reach a situation in which a series of negative or toxic thoughts accumulate, which can sow a restlessness that will consume us inside for a long time. That is why we must use our understanding, our intelligence, to know how to delimit that kind of thoughts, to know how to detect the ones that are really important for us.

In fact, it is a matter of avoiding confusion, which is caused by all those thoughts that take hold in our consciousness and that influence our judgments and opinions and the examination we make of reality when we look at what exists outside of us.

All that which is reproduced in our mind can hinder us, can contribute to our own suffering, if we become accustomed to navigate in those contents; many of which are closer to our own imagination than to reality, to truth.

We must be careful in our examination of the events that happen to us, for we can develop a series of unrealistic conclusions that can lock us into an invented world that bears no resemblance to the one that exists outside.

April 22, 2020

It is important what is produced in our mind, because everything that is created influences us in such a way that it can block us for long periods of time, especially if the thoughts that are established there are negative.

We are not aware of the influence that many mental contents have on us. If we were aware of this we would not allow them to dilate in time, we would immediately try to eliminate them from our consciousness as quickly as possible.

In the end we are the fruit of what we constantly think, of what is repeated most frequently. That is why we must be attentive and give the importance it deserves to all those elements that move tirelessly in that space, that always try to express something in some way and that come to influence us in such a way that they can alter our mood, our own emotions.

Without realizing it, we can be building a whole unreal world inside us, based on thoughts that we pay attention to and that try to dominate us more and more strongly. When a structure of thoughts is created around an irrational idea, negative for us, it can cause us great damage on an internal level; it can irritate us, create suffering and increase negativity in such a way that we can become paralyzed, not knowing what to do.

We cannot allow ourselves to be fooled by this mechanism. Sometimes we allow it to confuse us, to cause us suffering for no apparent reason. We cannot be paralyzed simply because a series of thoughts have taken hold of us. We must come to a certain control of what is produced there, of the contents that spread throughout our consciousness that try to force us to follow a certain direction.

We must not allow an idea to imprison us, a way of thinking to make us believe in lies and unreal fantasies that only exist in our own imagination. We must not allow a thought to lead us to sadness or cause us boredom. In those moments we must know that it is only an idea, a thought.

Our way of seeing reality also depends on the contents that we have in our mind at any given moment, on the mental structure that we create over time by repeating the same thoughts.

It is important that we know that our judgments, our reasoning and our vision of things can be very relative, because they depend on the kind of thoughts that predominate in each moment there. In such a way that, in another situation, in other circumstances, this may vary: we may even think the opposite of what we have thought at a previous moment. Mental movement is like that, it is contradictory, it depends a lot on the situation we are in and the circumstances we are experiencing.

April 23, 2020

With time and with the experiences that we accumulate, we learn something of how we function inside, how our mind works. Only those who have a great curiosity for these subjects can reach a superior knowledge, if they make an effort to observe themselves and analyze all those processes that take place there that are constantly conditioning us.

When we know ourselves we know the consequences that certain mental contents can have if we allow them to be repeated frequently, if we pay too much attention to them. We can anticipate what will happen if we insist on a certain thought; we can know this from experience, from what has happened to us on previous occasions.

If we know how to make a proper reading of everything that happens to us, we can avoid acting in the same way in the future, because we already know the consequences that insisting on a particular behavior can have for us. If we know our mental mechanism, we will know that before a behavior there is a thought, a mental content that leads us to perform that action. Therefore, we can anticipate our own behaviors if we really want to avoid them, and we can do so if we are aware of what is produced beforehand, because that is where the action we carry out starts.

This is only possible if we analyze our behaviors a little bit and detect the kind of contents that are behind them, that arise previously in our mind and prepare us to act in a certain direction. If we reach this level of analysis we will be able to put an end to many habits that may be altering our well-being, our mental health.

We have to be aware that everything always starts from there, from the same place, which is our mind. The origin is in all those contents that arise in it and to which we pay attention. If we insist on them, in the end they end up repeating themselves and subsequently have an effect on us.

It is an automatic movement over which we have hardly any control and it is very easy for it to be triggered or accelerated at any moment, and in those cases it is very difficult to stop it or change the direction of the thoughts that at that moment are sliding through our consciousness.

All this we must take into account if we really want to understand how our mind works, if we want to understand the reasons that make us behave in a certain way in some situations. Just by observing ourselves we will realize that this is the way this system works. It is a system that to have a certain control over it we must be very attentive to everything that transits in that space, because depending on the characteristics of the content that is in each moment there, so we will behave and will be our own emotions.

April 24, 2020

We are the fruit of our own mind. If we do nothing to control it, in the end it will determine us, because it has a great power over us. It has the power of our thinking, which has the power to guide us in a particular direction, so that if we are not aware of it we can do nothing to avoid it and in the end we end up making a choice simply because a series of thoughts have previously planned it in our consciousness.

This is how our mind works. Many procedures are produced mechanically, without us intervening too much through the use of our own will. Content is introduced little by little and becomes established there until it forms an idea that becomes so strong that in the end it leads us to a concrete action. If we want to find an explanation for everything we do, we only have to look at the kind of thoughts we have had previously, because those thoughts are the ones that have originated our behaviors, our way of acting and of facing the different situations we have to face.

This is how we function: we evolve to the extent that we draw conclusions from our own actions and we rectify by trial and error what we do; and this is then transferred to our thoughts, because they are based on all the information that we accumulate through our own experiences.

Our mind, in this way, is being perfected and each time we are obtaining more information that later will help us in the solution of problems, at the time of solving the difficulties that arise.

If we understand that this works this way, we will understand ourselves much better, we will understand why we act in a certain way on certain occasions. We will accept many mistakes made in the past, probably due to lack of information, to not having enough premises to know sufficiently what was the right decision at that moment.

Life is a continuous learning process that allows us to constantly have information that we store in our memory and that will remain there for when we need it. When the time comes, it will be reproduced in our mind and depending on the circumstances we will decide which option is the best for that situation.

Those people who have a greater capacity for analysis, or who have enhanced their capacity for reflection and reasoning, will undoubtedly make the best decisions, although they may also make mistakes. The person who is not used to analyze himself, to observe himself and to reflect a little on the consequences of his own behaviors, of his thoughts, is easy to make mistakes more often when making a decision, when choosing a particular path.

April 25, 2020

All your problems are over if you get to the source, if you get used to looking beyond and get to the bottom of what is really going on.

Everything that destroys you may be inside you. That's why you can't let yourself go, you can't neglect yourself. You have to establish an order, a balance within yourself to stop what is consuming you. You cannot just accept it. You must locate the origin of the suffering, somehow confirm the causes that are weakening you; it is the only way to master yourself; it is the only way to straighten out the problems that are trying to weaken you.

You cannot sink because of all those thoughts that rush through your mind, that cause you anguish and restlessness that lead you to emptiness in a hurry. You cannot let yourself be carried away by discouragement and despondency; you must establish a distance from your own mind. It is the way to banish all those thoughts that are articulated in your consciousness trying to divert you from reality; trying to make mistakes, leading you to error, disorder, confusion.

All your disorders begin there, when you give importance to illogical, irrational thoughts, when there is no interval on your part to separate yourself from what you are thinking, to eliminate in some way all those negative thoughts that are constantly appearing, trying to alter reality.

If you let yourself be surprised by all these elements, in the end you will find yourself a bit disoriented: you will not know how to find a way out and you will not be able to recover your true identity, your true self.

If you know how to maintain order within yourself, you will be able to lead a coherent life, close to your true purpose. You will destroy the unhappiness within you. You will be more awake and you will not allow everything that divides you inside to spread in your mind.

It is only a matter of isolating all those thoughts that try to dominate you. If you know how to distinguish them, you will be able to separate yourself from them, prevent them from altering you. It is about breaking that vicious circle that we compose within ourselves and that is so difficult to undo, because it does not stop. You remain paralyzed for long periods of time without offering any opposition on your part.

Many times we allow ourselves to be engulfed by this mechanism that separates us from ourselves and leads us to darkness; to reason without any logic; to design a fictitious reality that little by little imposes itself in that space until it extends throughout our consciousness and spreads into our own inner voice, where each and every one of our thoughts, everything that circulates through our consciousness, is disintegrated.

Without realizing it, we give continuity to a series of thoughts that try to sow pain and suffering in us. We allow all this because we allow ourselves to be deceived by our own mind, which sometimes works in an irrational way, when some false contents are installed in it that cause us affliction and from which we cannot free ourselves so easily.

April 26, 2020

I often transit from one thought to another. The quantity is not reduced, I simply keep going round and round with the same idea, sometimes in a disproportionate way, without any order.

This mental game, in many occasions, is consuming my time, when what I should be doing is to organize myself a little, to order my life a little.

The thing is that this mental game is not exhausted, it remains constant, associating some thoughts with others, in a continuous and excessive way. Sometimes I think I can conquer that part of my mind, where this happens. Sometimes I think that I am able to gather enough strength to acquire the necessary wisdom to fix all that mess that is distributed there in the form of ideas and thoughts.

Sometimes I think it's just a matter of knowing myself a little, knowing how I work. In this way I will be able to understand how these constant thoughts are concentrated in my consciousness, which sometimes provoke a revolution in me, since they guide me towards a certain action, often without me being aware of it.

I have always wanted to confront this process to try to dominate it, but surely there are things that I do not know, since when the first jolts of these thoughts begin I give myself to them quickly, and from there I observe that I find myself in a chain that does not end, that can be prolonged in time while I keep myself coiled in the same ideas, which in the end incite me to see life in a certain way.

I am convinced that it is possible to put an end to all these repetitive processes that occur in that space, the results of which are not always what I want. I believe that there must be some way to interrupt this mechanism, which in reality is nothing more than an unconscious habit that is produced within us and that we feed every day without realizing it.

I think it is important, to take a first step, to stay relaxed and start to see those thoughts that are illustrating our consciousness and that call our attention and awaken our interest and finally direct our behaviors.

In reality, these thoughts are the ones that mark the direction of our actions, in such a way that they determine us, unless they diminish or we manage to make them not so abundant.

I believe that, with a little willpower on our part, we can reach a certain balance within ourselves, in our inner self. I believe that we can make good decisions, as long as we isolate ourselves from what tries to contaminate us with all those ideas and contents that only sow difficulties in our conscience and create restlessness and make us live in uneasiness.

Sometimes it is just a simple thought that triggers this whole process that then begins to grow and spread throughout our consciousness, so that other thoughts arise and join with the previous ones and in the end this is what really ends up causing confusion, a disorder within us that can confuse us in such a way that we can gradually move away from reality; it is a process that is not easily eliminated.

For this we should be attentive to the moment in

which this occurs, to try to change a little the orientation of our thoughts, to disconnect in some way. If we manage to do so, tranquility and calmness will come to us, and perhaps it will be a good tool to achieve our own transformation.

If we manage to disarm that process, if we manage to establish an order, we will achieve clarity, balance; we will organize a little bit all those thoughts that confuse us and spread throughout the length and breadth of our consciousness.

April 27, 2020

What is represented in our mind is what is marking the way, what is ordering what we have to do in each moment. We can become conscious of these thoughts or simply let our mind decide for us, so we will act in this case in a mechanical, directed way, determined by this mechanism.

For us it is easier to obey than to take the reins of what happens in our consciousness. When we act in a mechanical way we already know the steps to follow, we already know the protocol, we do not have to make any effort to learn new behaviors or new steps to follow. It is much easier for us to act in this way, since we do not have to spend too much energy on learning new forms of behavior. Our actions are already automated, so that we repeat them automatically. That is why in many occasions we act like robots directed by a mental programming that we have been building ourselves over time, based on repeating over and over again the same behaviors, which are nothing more than the fruit of those thoughts that are repeated and spread in that space.

On the contrary, it is more difficult for us to stop and analyze a little bit that which is showing itself there and which is trying to determine us in some way. For us that means a greater effort, a greater expenditure of energy and we are not always willing to do that. The simple fact of stopping to observe ourselves already requires a change on our part to stop that mechanical way of acting that we often have. It is an effort for us, because we are not used to act that way. But with time it will be much more beneficial for us, we will see the results in everything we do, in our way of acting and being in the world, because we will act much more calmly, without doing things as impulsively as we often do. Our mind will no longer condition us so much.

Everything that happens in our mental space is then, in one way or another, reflected on the outside, in everything we do and say. Everything that happens there has an effect on us that can be seen on the outside, in our attitude towards life, in our habits and in many other things of which we are not aware.

We must make an effort to try to match what we really want to be with what is in our mind. We must identify our thoughts to see if they are related to what we are or what we want to be. If we find that there is a great distance between one thing and the other, then we will feel that there is no balance, that there is a great contradiction within us, because we will have the sensation that our thoughts do not correspond with what we really want to be, with what we want to do in life.

When there is not this correspondence we must reflect to find the way to achieve this balance, so that there are not so many contradictions within us, so that what we think corresponds to what we really want to do. It is a work of observation both externally, seeing what we do, and internally, taking into account what we think: the thoughts to which we are giving greater importance.

April 28, 2020

What makes us weak or what strengthens us is always exposed in our mind.

Sometimes we allow ourselves to be captivated by a series of strange thoughts that try to point us in a certain direction. If we know the process, we can get to expel this kind of contents that after all cause a disorder in the deepest part of ourselves. If we manage to push them away, they will disintegrate and the confusion, which at first may seem enormous, will eventually fragment and lose its influence over us.

We only have to pay a little interest to detect all those negative thoughts that try to deform reality, our vision of things or those contents that lead us to affliction, to sadness, that provoke a great imbalance in our internal world.

We must try to disassociate ourselves from all these elements that extend throughout our consciousness that, without us being very conscious of it, try to unbalance us, to move us away from reality and reason. Everything that happens there is of great importance. It can immobilize us, stagnate us. If they are not beneficial contents they can lead us to more problems.

That is why we must know how to deal with them,

know the role they play in our behaviors and in our actions, in our way of being. If we know the properties of many of the mental contents that are hidden in our consciousness, we will be able to manage them in a more effective way, to prevent them from leading us to madness.

We cannot neglect this task, we must strive to distinguish what causes us suffering, what hurts us and tries to impose itself in our mind over other kinds of contents. We must be attentive from the moment they are born until they disappear.

If we do it in this way, we will train our mind, even if only momentarily, and this will have good consequences for us, since we will decide at each moment the most appropriate content. We will establish, therefore, a mental order, where we will stop all those thoughts that do not suit us because they try to imprison us, to tie us in some way.

In this way we will be able to orient ourselves in a more effective way. We will not allow ourselves to be imprisoned by the influence of our mind, which sometimes entangles us in sufferings that it itself invents to try to increase, in this way, that chaotic movement of thoughts and images that little by little try to envelop us, because as they advance they occupy the whole extension of our consciousness.

If we pay attention to all that set of contents that try to impress us and we reach a certain control over them and we do not evade, we will reach true freedom. We will stop acting in an automatic way and everything will make more sense: both our thoughts and our actions. We will not waste time in the lethargy of confusion, because we will value other ways of understanding life.

Everything depends on our interest, on our curiosity to examine all that which extends there, sometimes without realizing it; it can destroy us if we do not distinguish it in due time.

We can achieve this control if we gain control of all that mental activity that never seems to end and is inflexible.

If we are calm and quiet enough to control all those unconscious impulses, in the form of thoughts, we can break many vicious circles to which we are accustomed. We will be able to moderate ourselves, control situations a little more and stop living under the servitude of everything that the mind proposes to us at every step.

April 29, 2020

When there are difficulties we must take control and direction, see what is weakening us and causing confusion. Surely it is because some mental contents have been imposed and have taken over our attention, they have become present in our consciousness, we have given them importance and somehow they are preventing us from being calm.

Many of our problems are produced by us through everything we think. We are obstinate in maintaining a series of ideas that in the long run do nothing more than confuse us, if we abandon ourselves to them.

The correct way to act is by deciding on our own thoughts, directing and controlling a little bit all those contents that are incorporated in our mind and that try to channel our attention towards a certain place, towards a specific way of thinking.

All this happens because we allow it: to the extent that we give importance to those thoughts, we feed them in some way. If we do not pay attention, that inner voice gradually dies out, all those thoughts that often overflow us are eliminated and stopped.

When we establish a pause we somehow stop that movement of contents that builds a certain way of thinking inside us, so we can intervene in that game that is established in that space. We can avoid associating some thoughts with others, when they are exposed there.

If we succeed, our thoughts will cease to have an intention and therefore will cease to influence us; they will not have a continuation, a stability; they will not remain for so long in our mind and will not be part of that internal chatter that we all have in which all those mental representations that arise at every moment accumulate. So the disorder, which is actually what causes us that uneasiness that we often feel, will disappear.

If we know how to explore within ourselves, we will verify all this; we will find a greater clarity that will help us to guide us correctly to do what we must do to be ourselves, to act in consonance with our true purpose.

Then our actions will be the extension of what we really want to do, we will not be inclined to follow what our mind dictates us in each moment.

Our reflections will have a more solid base, a greater foundation, because we will examine in more detail each thing we think, since we will be liberated from all those thoughts that many times pass through our mind that fill us with uncertainty because we do not know how to guess what their intention or true purpose is.

Many of these thoughts are so powerful that we do not have the capacity to stop them, so that in the end we allow ourselves to be governed by them.

Perhaps we are not prepared to face all these mental processes all the time, but we can try to look for that calm, that tranquility to manage in a more adequate way all those elements that ascend and descend through our mind following one after the other in a movement that takes place very quickly, so that we hardly have enough time to implement that necessary pause that provides us with a harmony that leads us to balance, temperance and good judgment.

May 1, 2020

Sometimes we try to join thoughts that can lead us to confusion, especially when they are linked to ideas and reasoning far from the truth. When this union is established between these elements that are not objective, it creates a message, a point of view, a belief that has nothing to do with reality, but quite the opposite: it projects even more confusion inside you.

Therefore, many contents that concur in your mind are not useful, because the only thing they do is to increase the disorder, the confusion that may be inside you.

In order to restore order, it is necessary to detect those incomprehensible thoughts that try to unite with each other and that separate us, often without being aware of it, from the reality that surrounds us.

It is therefore important to make good use of our understanding; to be aware at all times of all those processes that persevere, that try to become strong, but that in the end have no foundation, although they persist and are firm and try to form structures of thoughts uniting with each other.

We must put an end, in these cases, to this kind of processes that try to contaminate us by prolonging themselves in time, making us believe in a non-existent world or in a reality covered with setbacks, confusion and turbulences.

If we do not regulate this kind of mechanisms, restlessness will reign within us, suffering will envelop us and anguish will conquer us.

Everything begins in our judgments, in the prudence we have when associating what we observe and what we think at each moment. Everything must keep a coherence, a relationship. If we deviate too much from reality, when we try to examine it, we will form, through our subjective judgments, a different reality that in many cases may be distanced from the one that really exists.

It all depends on the way we reflect, on the way we order our thoughts. Depending on this, so will be the impressions that will be established in our mind, which will then be transformed into traces that will become part of our memory. Depending on how we interpret the world, what happens to us, we will achieve inner balance or not.

The destruction of oneself depends on what you think at any given moment. You are the one who determines the guidelines of your own thoughts, which try to show you the way, which show you a reality that sometimes may only exist in your mind.

Your way of thinking can lead you to error, to affliction, if it is not correct: if it is dominated by unreason.

That is why you should pay special attention to all those thoughts that live there, that expand in your consciousness trying to articulate a certain mental structure, which will order your vision of the world, your interpretation of things and everything that happens to you at every moment.

May 2, 2020

With a little effort on our part we can get results. Just by being aware of the importance of our mind in everything we do, in the way we behave, we already have a great advantage. We can only achieve this if we get used to being aware of everything we do and what we think. And the fact is that in many occasions we are only the effect, the consequence of the contents of our mind, especially when we simply obey the dictates of each thought that arises in that mental movement that never stops.

If we separate ourselves a little, if we manage to establish a distance with everything that is produced there, we will achieve greater freedom to decide for ourselves, to know which elements can harm us and which cannot. We can only achieve this if we are sufficiently observant and get used to pause a little to analyze what is there at that moment.

If we are in contact with that dimension where everything we are and everything we do is constituted, we will be able to establish modifications in time, before the manifestations that are established there determine us, before our mind takes total control and directs us, establishing the path we have to follow and what we must do in each moment.

Our main function, therefore, is to reach a control of that space, because it is there where our transformation begins: that change that in many occasions we need to see things differently, to solve the problems that in most cases we create ourselves by attending to a set of negative thoughts that without realizing it we feed for long periods of time.

If we get used to do this kind of exercise frequently, we will quickly see the results. We will see that our mind does not have as much influence as it seems to have over us, since we have several tools to reach a mastery over it, to make it work in a different way: with a little more order and in a less mechanical way.

But all this can only be achieved through practice, through continuous exercise, through the observation of ourselves especially at times when we find a certain tranquility around us and there are not too many stimuli that can distract us.

Then we will achieve a certain control. And we will also obtain enormous benefits in many ways: we will have greater clarity; our vision of things will be more objective and closer to the reality of life. It will also influence our decision making, when we have to choose between different options we will do it with greater precision; our decisions will be more objective.

In short, we will see life in a different way: with greater positivity and with a different attitude. We will feel freer, closer to what we really are. There will be greater coherence in everything we do and therefore we will be more satisfied with ourselves.

May 3, 2020

Every thought is a seed in our mind, since once it is planted there it can grow on its own. It can be nourished by other similar contents emerging from memory. Each thought has a life of its own, can spread far and wide in our mind autonomously, and can establish relationships with other related thoughts. When united with other similar thoughts, they form ideas that are then reflected in our reasoning, in our reflections.

Many thoughts can be there for long periods of time and then disappear, simply because there comes a time when a certain subject ceases to interest us; it is then replaced by another related to another subject that is also important to us for some reason.

Our mind is a mechanism, a constant movement that never stops. It is always trying to produce thoughts, to bring content to consciousness; it is always active, in one way or another.

Sometimes, when we observe ourselves and try to see what thoughts are in it, it may seem to us that it works in a slower way; in these cases we have the feeling that we can have a certain control.

It is a mechanism that tries to repeat very often the same contents, that is why we repeat so many times the same things, the same actions and the same reasonings, which form in most of the occasions vicious circles that we cannot stop. This usually happens when no new information is generated in that space, when for a time the contents that are established in it are always the same. When there are new elements, either because they have emerged from our memory or because we have introduced them voluntarily, the previous contents stop repeating themselves, giving way to new thoughts. This is how the mental mechanism works: it regenerates itself by changing some thoughts for others according to the new information that is introduced.

This is why we sometimes spend long periods of time always thinking about the same ideas, the same thoughts and the same problems. And it is because we are always focused on the same content, always handling the same information, without introducing new elements that can give a twist in the direction of this mental movement that is always revolving around the same information.

It is important and has a great effect on us the fact that we have a certain curiosity to learn new things, to introduce new information in our mind, because this enriches it and it is not always focused on the same topic, on the same issues. It is positive and beneficial that we teach our intellect to function in a different way, providing it with a variety of content and information so that its functioning is more complete, more enriching and effective.

When we are always focused on the same subject, our mind will only revolve around that subject; it will hardly get out of there. This influences and affects the decision-making process: when we have to choose between different options and we are not very clear about which path to choose. If we have become accustomed to always handling the same information, we will make decisions based on the information we have. If it is scarce because it has always been the same, it will not be very clear to us that this is the path to choose: we will lack security in our decisions, because we will always have the feeling that we lack information to be able to choose more effectively.

Therefore, whenever possible, we must provide our mind with a wide variety of content. We cannot always be thinking about the same things.

May 4, 2020

Everything that is represented in your mind makes you act in a certain way. The essential thing is what you think, what you end up doing is the fruit of that; it is a consequence of the thought that you have in each moment.

What exists in our mind is what makes us ready for action. Therefore, we must give this the importance it deserves, because depending on the contents that we have in our consciousness at each moment, so will be our actions, which are nothing more than a reflection of those elements that are in that space.

So, if we intend to change a certain behavior because we understand that it is not beneficial for us, we must first look at the kind of thoughts that we are promoting. That set of thoughts that are established there by repeating them over and over again is what makes it possible and forces us to behave in a certain way.

Therefore, if we want to change our behaviors we must first start by making changes in our way of thinking. It becomes necessary, in these cases, that we focus on other kinds of thoughts if we really want to change a particular behavior.

If there are changes in our mental representations,

there will also be changes in our actions, in the way we behave, in our behaviors. Because everything starts from there and then has an effect on what we do, on the behaviors we perform, which then, if we repeat them constantly, end up becoming our daily habits.

This is interesting to keep in mind because if we want to establish changes in our habits, we must begin by modifying our own thoughts, paying attention to other different thoughts, with other characteristics, that are more beneficial to us, because in the end they will also end up becoming actions, behaviors.

To try to make changes in all those thoughts that then influence our behaviors, we must first take into account the usefulness of what we do, of what we repeat habitually. If we see that they are behaviors that do not lead us anywhere, that make us waste time and energy, it is advisable that we at least try to make changes to implement other more beneficial behaviors, which are more useful for us, for the objectives we are pursuing.

But where we have to start first is with the kind of thoughts that take place in our mind and that are repeated over and over again until they force us to act in a certain way. That is where we have to make sure that we make the appropriate changes, because those changes will then have their effect on our habits.

Our main objective, therefore, is our way of thinking. We must know ourselves to know why we pay attention to one kind of thinking and not to others; why we pay attention to a particular kind of content and have no interest in a different kind of element. Everything has to do with what interests us at any given moment, with what we pay attention to. We must know ourselves well to know why we pay attention to certain matters and not to others, to know what is behind it all; why we have a special interest in certain subjects and not in others. Only he who knows himself well can know the answer.

If we strip ourselves of everything that distracts us and focus on what we often think about, we will understand much better this movement of the mind that focuses only on certain thoughts and not on others; we will understand, among other things, how this whole process that ends up in our behaviors, in our behaviors, begins.

If we go to the origin, we can establish the appropriate modifications to change the direction of our own actions, since we will be able to stop certain thoughts from growing, from spreading throughout our consciousness. But this is only possible if we know ourselves, if we know the reasons that lead us to insist on a particular thought, or a set of thoughts. It is only possible if we go a little further and see what is behind all that mental movement that we have habitually in which a kind of thoughts are repeated over and over again in such a way that they force us to act in a particular direction, at the same time forming habits in us that then over time, once they take root, are difficult to eliminate.

May 5, 2020

Everything that spreads in our mind can determine us if we allow it, if we give it time to repeat itself over and over again and leave it to its free will. If we allow this then it will have consequences for us: we will act in an automatic way, conditioned by all those thoughts that are represented there and that do not stop repeating themselves.

Our behaviors, in this sense, are nothing more than the consequence of all those contents that are manifested in that space, which determine us if we are not aware of their influence.

The mind is an automatic system, but we can reach a certain control over it if we know how it works and we are aware of the processes that take place there. Then we can govern in a certain way this mechanism that in many occasions goes against our own interests, because it forces us to act in a way that we do not really want; because later, when we are conscious of our acts, many times we regret what we have done, and all this is because we have not been conscious of our behaviors that have been derived from a series of contents that have been exposed in a repetitive way in that space.

We can create real vicious circles that only serve to constantly repeat certain thoughts. For our mind this is a saving of energy because those thoughts are habitual and do not require an extra effort because it is already accustomed to that kind of thoughts and does not have to analyze them or place them in a category. You don't need to spend energy on these functions because those thoughts are already familiar, they are known, they are not new. This is the reason why thoughts tend to repeat themselves; it is for the simple saving of energy.

But this repetition can be harmful to us to the extent that they are toxic or negative thoughts. Because if they are so, they establish themselves very strongly and then it is very difficult to move them away from there. If they remain too long they can easily create in us a negative mentality. This is what explains the suffering that we often experience: it is because a series of thoughts take root there from so many manifestations; they gain strength in such a way that in the end they end up influencing our emotions, our state of mind.

The proof is that this suffering, or this anguish that we often feel, diminishes in intensity when we pay attention to other kinds of different thoughts. Then other different contents begin to represent themselves in our mind, replacing the previous ones. When this happens we are not aware that by the simple fact of changing our thoughts we have provoked a certain change in our mental structure, in the direction of some mental contents that were developing negative emotions in us.

If we want to take control of ourselves, therefore, we must first be aware of what we think, knowing that many thoughts have a great influence on everything we do; and, secondly, we can establish changes in the direction of what we think if we manage to put our focus of attention on other kinds of different thoughts. Then we will see changes in the functioning of our own mind, which will subsequently be reflected in our behaviors, in everything we do in our daily lives.

May 6, 2020

Our consciousness is a field that we should cultivate in a different way, trying to give permanence only to those thoughts that are in consonance with what we really want to do, with what we want to be. We should not allow other kinds of thoughts to be stored there, to start to become strong within our own mind. We must not deceive ourselves, let ourselves be confused by that movement that takes place within us that makes us interpret reality in a certain way; sometimes in a wrong way.

We must protect ourselves from many toxic thoughts, from many thoughts that are worthless and that remain in our consciousness for a long time, replacing other kinds of thoughts that are more positive for us.

We must discard that which does not serve us, refresh our intellect a little, add clarity to our consciousness. We cannot allow it to be covered with negative thoughts; because, if this kind of contents become frequent, we will follow the current of suffering and darkness; we will not find a way out of our problems, since this kind of thoughts in the end confuse us, increase our own disorders and do not help us to find alternatives; they will not let us keep walking forward.

There are thoughts that block us; they plunge us into deception and shadows. Those thoughts can dwell there, occupy a space if we allow it, if we only pay attention to that kind of contents and not to others; this makes them grow strongly.

We must be vigilant and pay special attention to everything that happens in that space, because in reality we are the consequence of everything that is produced there. Everything starts from our mind; everything starts there.

May 7, 2020

We are always looking for something. There are those who manage to penetrate a little more into the secrets that lie within and move away from the confusion of the mind, and manage to move and advance through that space where nothing stops.

There are those who manage to discover many things about themselves when they observe themselves, in spite of the abundance of contents that exist throughout the entire extension that is the consciousness, in spite of the fact that many elements appear disordered and are difficult to interpret.

There are those who manage to decipher all these representations, in such a way that they come to understand the origin of their suffering, of their anguish. Just by watching the course of his thoughts he manages to discover the cause of his affliction, he does not allow himself to be dominated by the course of his mind, nor does he abandon himself to what it proposes at every instant; his interest is rather in discovering how the activity of his consciousness is: how certain thoughts are grouped together and join with others until they finally create a certain vision of reality that marks what that person is at each moment.

Everything is based on the movement of the mind and what happens in it at each moment. Everything is limited to what we think, since in the end that is what ends up becoming action, in our behaviors, which in the end are what determine what we are at every moment.

If we want to achieve true transformation, we must change our focus. We have to focus more on what is happening inside us, on all those contents that try to organize themselves so that in the end you have a certain vision of the world; so that you reach conclusions about life and everything that has happened to you over time, and about each of your experiences. Based on these judgments, you will understand life in a particular way, you will end up having a certain point of view about many things that happen around you. This will give you the ability to make decisions when you have to face the various difficulties that you will experience throughout your life.

Depending on the conclusions you have drawn from all that has happened to you, so will be your decisions when facing your own problems. If your reflections are in line with reality, you will easily find the light, the solutions to each and every one of the difficulties you encounter.

If, on the contrary, your judgments are far from reality, there will exist in you a great discrepancy and many of the things that happen to you you will see them incongruent and you will not know how to find out the causes of your perturbation. Although you dedicate yourself to look for solutions you will not find them, due to the ignorance of what you are, of your inner functioning. In the end you will act in a compulsive way, because you will let yourself be contaminated by the first thing you think about everything that happens to you.

Your mind will configure you as it pleases, without any opposition from you, if in the end you allow yourself to be dominated by it. Your decisions will not always be the right ones. You will always be accompanied by a feeling of incoherence, because you will experience that you are not yourself in any action you take. You will have the conviction that you are letting yourself be carried away by your own thoughts and not by what you would really like to be or do at any given moment.

May 8, 2020

It is up to us to change the course of those thoughts that live in our mind, because we are in charge of cultivating them without realizing it. They are loaded one after another there and remain there for a while until the direction of our attention is changed, so that our mind focuses on another different objective.

If we understand that this works in this way, we can manage to transform this mechanism that in many occasions causes us restlessness, by the alternation of thoughts that create disturbance and that in many occasions escape from our control. Understanding that this works this way is a way to try to control this mechanism.

Although we can change the direction of those thoughts; we can manage to divert the focus of our attention to another place with a little willpower; we can change the line of our own thoughts. It is just a matter of being attentive, of using our attention when we need to proceed in this way.

It is a way to manage our own mind, especially in those moments when we need it, because we feel sad or when we have the feeling that there is an internal conflict. In those moments we can do this kind of practice, because, in fact, our mental darkness starts from there, it uses this mechanism.

May 9, 2020

Sometimes we do not see the light, all our thoughts move towards the same point, a black and dark point formed by negative thoughts that take over us and do not stop emitting. In this state we are inclined to do nothing, not to restore normality, clarity. We let ourselves be carried away by this tendency that has only one purpose, which is to sow negativity in all our ideas and projects.

If we are attentive we will clearly see how all these thoughts are grouped together, so that in the end they lead us to have a negative conception of the world, of the reality that surrounds us. Our mental representations, therefore, are filled with negativity, in such a way that they block the execution of our behaviors and we do not find the way out of that situation.

If we are aware that this works this way, if we reflect a little and we are conscious of this movement that many times takes place in our mind, we can establish solutions, choosing another kind of thoughts and affirmations a little more positive, until they begin to prolong in that space.

This is the only way to grow mentally. If we remain for too long under the negative effects of all those thoughts that often accompany us, we will feel blocked, with the feeling that we are always in the same place and that we never move forward. If we remain in the blockage we will be condemned to failure in all those things we want to do.

When we find ourselves in this situation and we recognize that within us there is something that does not work, that we are under the domination of a large number of toxic and negative thoughts that try to express themselves over and over again, we must make the determination to establish changes within ourselves, shifting our attention to other more positive, more beneficial matters. It is just a matter of making a small effort to redirect our mind, in this way we will also see its effects in our own behaviors.

It is good that we get used to establish a communication with ourselves, so that somehow we have some control over what we think. It is good that we keep an eye on that conversation that we often have in the depths of our inner world; that inner dialogue that we often have, which tells us what we have to think about next, what we should do in each situation.

We must be aware that everything that is built in that space influences our well-being. Our suffering always starts from there; all our conflicts and confusions and the darkness that many times is integrated in our consciousness in such a way that it clouds our reason.

Any thought, no matter how small, always has an influence, for better or for worse. In our mind is where everything is first organized: what we do, what we think, the decisions we make and even the way we behave when relating to others. Everything is presented there first. Every judgment we make about those things we see, about the situations we experience, is first produced there, where different thoughts combine to give rise to a reflection, a conclusion and a point of view.

May 10, 2020

There are many thoughts that are prolonged in time,

in such a way that they conquer us little by little. We become more and more aware of them and therefore they increase their power over us. They manage to reach such a strength that most of our ideas are related to those thoughts, every time we reflect or think about some matter.

Our thoughts are the beginning of everything, depending on their duration they will be so important. In the end, thoughts become actions that we repeat according to the constancy of those thoughts in that space. A set of actions forms a concrete activity and the repetition of this activity becomes a habit if we repeat it frequently. Once a habit has been established, it is very difficult to eliminate it.

Therefore, we must take into account what is established there, because it is the origin of our actions, of our activities and habits that mark a specific direction. If this direction that we take is positive for us there is nothing to worry about, but if we acquire negative habits we must contemplate the possibility of establishing some changes.

For the realization of these changes we must first count on our will, once we are aware of what we want to change. With a little effort on our part we can realize where is the origin of our conflicts, of our difficulties, and once we have detected the cause we can establish some solutions to change the course of our problems.

We must look, first of all, at what we are constantly repeating, because that is what is causing a particular habit. If we become aware of our own behaviors and the consequences they bring, we can gain some control over them. We have the capacity to be able to change them for healthier ones; it is the only possible procedure to eliminate all those habits that are trying to take us in the wrong direction.

If we look inside ourselves we will find the answers we need, we will find the causes that limit us, in such a way that we can distinguish all those harmful thoughts that are operating in that space without any opposition from us. It is only a matter of examining our consciousness; in this way we will see clearly what is manifested there and we can change it if we understand that these kinds of contents are not good for us.

Then it will change the direction of our life, of what we do constantly, day by day. So as time goes by we will see the changes that will take place in our way of thinking and in our own habits.

May 11, 2020

That which manifests itself in our mind has a lot of strength, it can lead us to a constant action if that content is important to us. When we repeat an action it becomes an activity that subsequently begins to form part of a habit. Our mind, therefore, has the capacity to create habits; this is why it totally dominates us.

Some habits may be beneficial to us and some may not. When we are dominated by unhealthy habits, we have the opportunity to change or eliminate them. We only need to pay attention to the behaviors that we repeat the most, because those are the ones that make us maintain that habit over time.

It is only a matter of focusing on other kinds of behaviors, that we make the effort to repeat them until they replace the previous ones. Habits are eliminated or modified when we manage to repeat other different behaviors.

Intervening on our own behaviors and establishing changes can be easy, because our own behaviors are visible to us. It is easy for us to become aware of what we do or do not do at a given moment and the consequences that this may have for us.

On the other hand, if we try to intervene on the functioning of our own mind this is more complicated, because it is a very fast movement, it is done unconsciously and there are less possibilities to control it.

We only feel the need to change it when we see its effects in our own life, in our habits and behaviors, in our circumstances; then we try to make an effort to think differently, but we see that it is not so easy because possibly our thoughts have been cultivated over a long time and have been developed by force of repeating them over and over again.

On the contrary, it is easier for us to identify our behaviors, what we do every day, from the moment we get up to the moment we go to bed. At the end of the day we usually make a review of what we have done and depending on the result of that review we feel satisfied with ourselves or not. When we do not feel satisfied we try to find out the reason and we propose for the next day to make some changes to try to modify that dynamic.

Even if we encounter the difficulty of having to change our own behaviors, it is always easier for us than intervening in our own mind to try to control some thoughts that spread through our consciousness and are negative for us.

Our own behaviors can be measured more easily

than the thoughts that give rise to them. It is easier to establish order in our behaviors than in all those elements that move unchecked throughout our mental space.

May 12, 2020

The path that the mind takes, when we let it act on its own, is the fastest. Whatever option is available to it is good, because it does not waste too much time worrying about the consequences of that option.

When we act impulsively, we are guided solely and exclusively by it. On the other hand, when a decision is the result of reflection and deep reasoning, here we could say that there is a greater intervention on our part, because we voluntarily decide not to act at first, not doing the first thing that comes to our head.

When we intervene in this way on our mind, leaving time for reflection before performing a particular action, our decisions seem to have more weight, more chances of succeeding. If we act impulsively, it may in some cases be the best thing we can do, but it is also possible that many of our decisions are wrong.

It is not a bad thing to stop, even for a moment, before acting or making a decision. It is advisable to have at least a moment to predict the consequences of acting in a certain way. We can fall into the trap of acting impulsively, of doing the first thing our mind tells us to do, just like that.

We will feel more secure with ourselves if our actions are born from reflection. Everything we do then has consequences for us, they can be positive or negative. Therefore, it will always be beneficial to analyze the situation a little before acting. Many mistakes we make in life come precisely from here, from this point. It is necessary to put ourselves in the situation in which we find ourselves in order to act in a way that is in accordance with that specific circumstance. All this can be considered if we pause briefly before acting and do not do the first thing that comes to our mind.

When we make a mistake because we have acted impulsively, later, when we evaluate ourselves and look for an explanation for our mistake, we realize that we could have acted differently. But we do this exercise later and not at the precise moment. We are not used to this habit, to take into account the reality of the moment and the kind of thoughts we have in our minds before behaving in a certain way.

All this we can learn over time, by dint of practice. It can be a good way to eliminate our impulsivity, to avoid that it is only our mind that directs us, that decides for us. We must learn to intervene more, to be more attentive to what we do, to what we think, since this can avoid us numerous problems in the future.

It is only a matter of learning it through practice, through the exercise of observing ourselves, of observing our thoughts, being aware of the consequences that may arise if we constantly insist on a certain type of content. We must know that we are the product of our mind, that everything that manifests there then has consequences for us, in our behaviors, in our attitude and in the way we relate to others.

We have to learn to establish a certain control over it, and this would be a way to do it. It is a matter of us doing this exercise frequently, this practice of stopping briefly, being aware of what we are thinking, before making a decision or carrying out a particular behavior or action. It would be a way of being in the world as more conscious, with greater control over ourselves.

If we get used to act in this way we will have much more facilities to make the right decisions. We would not make so many mistakes nor would so many negative habits be implanted in us that later are so difficult to eradicate, when we realize that they are not beneficial.

Our mind is a system that we have to learn to master somehow. The first step to achieve it is to know it, to analyze its functioning, being aware of the influence that these processes have on us, on what we do, on the kind of thoughts we have and on our own emotions, on our state of mind.

It is a very useful tool, but if we use it properly. It can turn against us, having quite a few negative effects on us, if we do not use it properly, if we let ourselves be carried away by the direction it is leading us in each moment.

May 15, 2020

Many times we live in bewilderment because of small contradictions that we have within ourselves. Here our work should consist in analyzing what is provoking a conflict in our mind, for surely it is what is destroying us at that moment. Once we are aware that there is no clarity, we can begin to consider the contents that are causing us this confusion.

We have to be aware that in our mind there are many contradictions. We can attend to a thought that goes in a certain direction and in a short period of time we can deviate towards another totally opposite one. We can think one thing and the opposite almost at the same time. Our mind is a source of constant contradiction, especially when we have doubts about what action to take in a given situation.

Perhaps at that moment we need time to make the right decision, but we do not always have this opportunity to delay an action. Sometimes circumstances require us to act with determination and at that very moment. Many times we cannot stop to evaluate the consequences of a particular act, of a particular decision. It is through time that we can observe the consequences of many of our actions, of many decisions we have made in the past.

When we are aware of the consequences of our own actions, then we make a reading and draw conclusions. It is like an evaluation that we make to ourselves that somehow helps us to act more effectively in the future, as long as we make the correct reading, since it is not always so, we do not always extract a positive reading of what happens to us.

Depending on the reading we make of the events that happen to us, the quality of the information will be incorporated into our memory and will be there for when we need it: when it is our turn to live a similar circumstance.

That is why it is important that we know how to reflect and draw our own conclusions from everything that happens to us. It will be valuable information for us that in time will manifest itself to help us to solve some difficulties that we may have at some point.

For all this it is important that we are good observers of everything that happens around us, of what happens in our daily life. From everything we can draw a reading, a conclusion, a reflection that will be stored there and that will appear in the future.

All the information that we get from our own experiences, from the observation that we make of the reality that surrounds us, is very important for our survival, to manage in life and in the world that we live in. The more experiences we have in life, the more complete will be all the information we need to solve our own conflicts.

That is why it is important to pay attention to everything that happens to us, even to all those processes that take place within us, in our own internal dialogue. There is also all that information that we have stored in our memory and that is constantly emerging, constituting in each moment a vision of reality, a vision of our own life.

Our reasoning and decisions depend on all that stored information, which is nothing more than the consequence of the reading we have made of our own past experiences. All these contents have been stored in our memory and through the movement of our own mind emerges in our consciousness. At that moment we can observe those contents and decide which one is the most appropriate for the situation we are in.

May 16, 2020

When we become hooked on a thought we become trapped: we then have great difficulty in detaching ourselves from it when it becomes established in our mind over a long period of time.

Our mental representations, once they settle in, are

difficult to get rid of. To do this we must put other, different thoughts in their place, and this takes time and dedication. This can be achieved consciously, through the use of our will; or this change is accomplished little by little over time, as we replace one kind of thought with another.

If we know that this is the procedure that our mind uses, we will understand ourselves much better, we will understand many actions and habits that we have been acquiring over time. This is how this mechanism works. Whenever certain thoughts gain prominence they begin to repeat themselves and then it is very difficult to remove them from there.

These thoughts, as they gain strength, involve us more and get us to perform a series of actions almost without realizing it. These actions, once we repeat them over time, become habits that we carry out without being aware of the consequences.

When something significant happens to us then we look at ourselves, we look inside ourselves to look for a cause. When it is something important we try to look for the reasons that have led us there to try to prevent it from happening again in the future. We look both outside and inside ourselves to find a convincing explanation as to what caused the situation.

We only stop to reflect a little when certain things happen to us, when this should be more common. We should get into the habit, through the use of our own will, of stopping from time to time to try to find out what issues are most frequently occupying that space, what kind of thoughts are being represented in it. Then we will understand many situations that we habitually live; our way of behaving with others and our way of seeing the reality that surrounds us.

May 17, 2020

It is important that there is order within us. There is a constant activity in our brain that we cannot stop, but we can become aware of what we are thinking, of what at a particular moment is manifesting in our consciousness. From this capacity we have to be aware we can obtain great information about ourselves, about how our mind works and the kind of thoughts to which we pay more attention.

Although we lack the tools and means to keep everything in perfect order, we can achieve a certain control of our thinking through meditation.

When we meditate we stop to observe what happens in that space, we see the images that at that moment circulate through our consciousness and we can analyze in a more detailed way the thoughts, as well as that internal conversation that we have with ourselves, which is our inner voice that manifests itself in an internal dialogue where all those thoughts that are emerging there are detached.

Thanks to meditation we can decompose many contents that are represented in our consciousness; we can focus more on every detail; we can look for the causes of what is happening to us. If we do not stop we hardly have time to find the explanations we need to understand ourselves.

It is a matter of looking for a meaning to everything that happens inside us. To do so, all we need to do is to reflect a little, to get away from that mental noise in which the same thoughts are constantly repeated.

May 18, 2020

Seeking tranquility helps me when I am too accelerated; in those moments, where one is more active, it is difficult to make the best decisions, to distinguish what is better or worse.

Calmness, silence, provides that ability to discern in a more objective way, especially when many ideas pile up in your head and you can't get closer to the truth. For all these reasons it is important that we cultivate the art of calm, silence and temperance.

We can only achieve this if we isolate ourselves a little from the external noise that contaminates us in some way, and which is usually frequent, so that we have become accustomed to it and we allow ourselves to be absorbed by its surprising power, by its influence. We allow ourselves to be attracted by all those external stimuli that we find around us.

Peace, tranquility, manages to unite all that is separated. When we achieve it, that feeling of calmness spreads throughout our body; we begin to be more conscious and we do not allow ourselves to be dragged by all those impulses that arise from deep within us and that try to guide us many times towards confusion.

When we are in silence, in calm, some elements that create disorder disappear; this is one of the advantages. Many of the thoughts that repeat themselves in our mind, that try to drill us constantly, repeating themselves over and over again, cease to be frequent. In this way we experience a well-being that makes us a little happier in those small instants. It is as if we move away from our irrational mind to another dimension where we see everything with a little more clarity, far from all those interpretations that we often make of everything that goes through our heads at any given moment.

In silence we also have thoughts, but this helps us to penetrate something more, at a deeper level, where we find an illumination that makes us see clearly where the deception of our own mind is. It allows us to observe how our thoughts march one after the other, how they move along our consciousness.

By the simple fact of being aware of this, we manage to establish a distance, in such a way that all those mental contents stop influencing us; at the same time they stop remaining there, they stop repeating themselves, they stop reproducing themselves. We can only achieve this if we establish this distance through silence.

All those elements that are in that space can become overwhelming, because they do not stop. They always try to show themselves through representations that often disfigure the reality we observe outside, so it is important that we always try to seek order. It is necessary that we put a stop to everything that tries to consume our energy in matters that do not lead anywhere.

The best path is always silence. It is where that inner light dwells that we must never lose, that makes us appreciate the purity of things. It is the best way not to be subordinated to this mechanism, not to be subjected to all that it is proposing to us at every step.

Only from serenity we can observe all that is hidden inside; we can concentrate on what we really are; we can approach the truth, the objectivity of things; we can see life in a simpler way, away from the pressure of all those misleading thoughts that tend to sprout in our mind in a constant, successive way, in a movement that tries to separate us from what we really are.

May 20, 2020

We must pay attention in more detail to many thoughts that we have and that are not beneficial to us, because they come loaded with confusion and disorder, or are toxic and do not make us move in the right direction.

If through the use of our will we manage to be attentive to all that is agitated in our mind, that moves in our consciousness, we can diminish the effect that it can have on us, because we can avoid that it determines us; we can stop that influence.

If we establish an interval before acting, we will verify that, in reality, what we are going to do is to follow what our mind is dictating to us at that moment. Then we can realize, in that brief space of time, if what we are going to do has some benefit or instead the only thing it leads to is a waste of time or an unnecessary waste of energy.

All the elements that arise in our mind coming from our memory are the fuel by which this one feeds, reason why it is important to discover the type of contents that occupy it. If there is an excess of negative, toxic contents, in the end we will end up acting in the wrong direction. We will do things that we will later regret, when we realize that all those things we have done have actually led us nowhere.

May 21, 2020

Sometimes you let yourself be cornered by some thoughts that isolate you from reality, that make you weaker, that overwhelm you and lead you to deep discouragement. And you can hardly protect yourself, you feel how your mind becomes clouded and very briefly you start to be overwhelmed by a series of ideas that absorb you little by little.

Whenever we concentrate on a series of thoughts, we usually allow ourselves to be seduced by them and allow it to settle there for long periods of time; we allow it, just like that.

If we focus on observing this mechanism that causes these thoughts to spread, with a little willpower, we would get used to protect ourselves a little more from everything that accumulates in our consciousness and that with time causes us a condition that is associated with another until in the end it causes us a series of disorders.

And all this is because we allow some contents to take over our attention, to take over our consciousness without us realizing it.

There is a way to prevent all this: it is by observing ourselves a little more, evaluating a little more what we think at certain times about what surrounds us.

If we manage to have this skill, we will not allow some negative thoughts to develop further in our mind. In this way our internal disorder will not increase and we will not let ourselves be carried away by all those stimuli that come from our unconscious, penetrating into that space with the idea of expanding in a movement that will slowly disturb us.

If we pay attention to all that is produced there and we are vigilant in some way, we will not allow confusion to take hold of us through all those impulses that take over our consciousness and that practically occupy the totality of our mind.

It is not easy to appease our thoughts; to avoid the confusion that many times they produce in us. The usual thing is that we allow ourselves to be subjected to all these processes that extend inside us and that are agitating us inside.

If the movement of our mind is negative, it can consume us little by little. If we allow it to advance and we do not anticipate it, in the end it will spread within us a suffering that is impossible to repress.

If we do not take the reins in due time, an unhappiness will be established within us that will slowly beat us, in such a way that we will not know how to manage it. We will simply be content to accept it without further ado, without any inclination on our part to try to change it.

If, on the other hand, we try to calm our mind, we will manage to organize all those contents that are hidden in our conscience, to reach the mastery of our own mental mechanism. When we achieve this, our doubts will disappear and all that overwhelm that often divides us seems as if it were suspended.

We can achieve all this through stillness, from that tranquility, where we can observe ourselves, to the point that we can decide whether or not to move away from certain thoughts, from all those ideas that somehow are robbing us of our own freedom. When we achieve this, we reach a harmony that makes us discover the truth.

May 22, 2020

Transformation begins with calm. From there you can identify the nature of your thoughts at any time. You can designate what is beneficial or not for you and you can pave the way to change what you desire: all those contents that you have become accustomed to over time and that have determined you without you being aware of it.

No matter how many thoughts you have in your mind, if you make a pause for that mechanism to stop, the magnitude of everything you are thinking will fade away. It does not mean that you are going to think about something else at that moment, what happens is that the effect of the thoughts diminishes on you.

This is why it is important to observe yourself; to look, from calmness, at what is happening. If you are aware of what is happening deep inside yourself, you will be able to find solutions, analyze your situation in a more complete, more objective way, and therefore you will be able to establish changes and other alternatives to solve those problems you have at that moment.

It is the only way to reach a control over all those elements that are presented again and again in your mind, which often accelerate without your consent, without you being very aware of it. If you approach to observe calmly all that is taking place there, you will be able to order a little the chaos that sometimes reigns inside you.

When you order your mind, you reach understanding, you discover the causes that have led you to be the way you are. At that moment is when you can make the best decisions, since in your mind there is clarity and in your conscience appear the best possible options to solve the difficulties.

Everything is in your head. If you concentrate on analyzing what you are thinking, you will realize that many thoughts try to multiply automatically. If you examine it closely you will realize that it is an operation, a movement that seems to have no end, unless you are conscious and focus on other kinds of thoughts. In such a case you can vary the course and get some of the contents that determine you to stop doing so, many thoughts that remain there constantly cease to be important and are changed by others that will gradually be introduced in that space.

If we do the exercise of analyzing the characteristics of our own thoughts and why they remain there for long periods of time, we will realize that those that occupy the most space are contents to which we have given great importance for some reason. For some reason they are significant for us and therefore they spread throughout our consciousness and develop a set of ideas, a way of understanding the world that directs us along a certain path.

May 23, 2020

Everything that is projected in your mind determines you in some way; it is difficult to separate yourself from it. The easy thing to do is to go along with whatever it dictates. We are accustomed to act that way. All the contents that penetrate our consciousness move us from one side to the other, inciting us to act in a certain direction.

We abandon ourselves to this involuntary and unconscious mechanism, without questioning the consequences of acting in a specific way or paying attention to a series of specific thoughts.

Our mind is what in some way sets the direction, without us often being aware of this process, of this mechanism that never rests.

We get lost in the bustle that is in it, in that movement where an immense amount of thoughts are constantly being articulated, which somehow help us to understand reality and to find the reasons why we can explain to ourselves what is happening; although sometimes we find it difficult to fully understand many circumstances we live.

When in our mind there is less noise, when it seems to be quieter, a calmness is released within us that somehow separates us from all that constant hustle and bustle to which we are normally accustomed. In those moments we feel that our understanding is more authentic, more objective.

It seems that tranquility, silence and calm help to dissolve a large number of contents, of thoughts that are there constantly.

When we manage to reach those moments, it seems to clear a little more, it seems that clarity makes its way thanks to the silence. Everything becomes easier to understand and at the same time we experience that the mind ceases to have that great dominion over us. In these cases we can achieve a greater depth in our reflections. We can go a little further, get to that other space where we reach a greater clarity.

When we are immersed in the noise of the mind, everything seems darker, more confusing. It is just a matter of freeing ourselves a little from that movement, from that confusion.

We must try to look for those moments of silence, of calm, to take control again in some way, to find moderation and to move away from all that disorder, from all that confusion that often circulates in that space that is moving us away from what we really are.

Our internal functioning will be much more adequate, we will have time to examine the progress of our own thoughts, of our ideas. We will be able to analyze in a more detailed way what happens to us. We will not feel the need to be constantly running from one place to another. It will help us to be more objective and more authentic.

If we get used to acting in this way, calmness will increase within us and this will be transferred to our own judgments, which will be more sensible; to our own reasoning, which will be more correct.

In this way we will be able to reflect and come to understand much better the reality that surrounds us, which many times confuses us, when the stimuli that surround us are very abundant.

May 24, 2020

All our answers are in the mind, it is only a matter of looking for the information we need to know. The solution to our problems is also there, we just have to clear out what does not serve us, what hinders our vision of things. Then order is established and we are able to find a way out of our difficulties.

There are times when we have greater clarity when making decisions, and there are other times when we are not so enlightened, it seems as if we have a blockage that obscures everything. In those moments we need to give ourselves some time for our mind to calm down, for certain thoughts to stop manifesting and occupying all that space that is our consciousness.

Only if we establish a time to give ourselves a little pause, we will stop feeling the pressure that comes from that space, from all those thoughts that try to rule us at every moment. When we achieve this we stop being under the effects of the mind and we start to have some control in some way.

To intervene in this way we need a little willpower on our part, understanding that this mechanism works in an automatic way, in such a way that many times it will lead us in a direction we do not want. That is why it is important to stop a little, to notice in those moments what we are thinking, what ideas we are paying attention to in those moments, and from there to take control of the situation, putting a little order within ourselves.

May 25, 2020

Not everything that occurs in our mind is important to us. We must select the elements that most interest us at each moment, but we do not always do so because the movement of the mind is very fast and we hardly have time to distinguish what really matters in each circumstance.

When we stop to analyze what we are thinking, we do find it easier to separate unnecessary thoughts from those that are useful to us. We can distinguish the contents that are not useful and those that can be useful to us at any given moment.

The point is to stop, even for a short time, to be able to orient our thoughts and many ideas that are represented in that place. It is about achieving a certain inner calm to put some order in all those elements that are in our consciousness and that try to build a certain reality many times without our conscious participation.

It is only a matter of paying attention to all those thoughts that stand out and that do not cease to occur in that space. When we have them localized it is easier to achieve a certain control over them, to put a minimum of order in all those ideas that crowd one after the other that in many occasions lead us to confusion.

When we are quiet, calm, our mind also experiences that stillness, so it decreases its intensity. It is as if it worked in a slower way, as if the strength of many thoughts diminishes and they do not have so much influence over us, so much power. Only in these cases we can reach a certain control over that space, which is used to work in a very fast way, constantly associating thoughts and ideas in a mechanical way.

Only in this case we can distinguish those thoughts that manifest themselves repeatedly. It is there where we must pay our attention, because those thoughts are the ones that are subsequently building our actions; they are the ones that are marking a tendency for us to act in a certain way at a particular time.

If we get used to observe our mind from tranquility, from calmness, an immense field of action opens up where we can intervene to get closer to what we really are, to what we really want to do. It is as if a space opens up so that we can intervene directly, in a conscious way, on what we think, on the contents that at that moment are in our consciousness.

Therefore, from calmness it is possible to reach a certain mastery of this mechanism, since its activity is less intense and we can detect more easily the thoughts that try to dominate us, that try to determine our behaviors and our habits.

If you observe yourself, calmly, for a long time, you will realize that your mind often acts in a disorderly way, it is like an uncontrolled current that takes you where it decides that you have to go. You will realize that it is a space where confusion often reigns, because one thought after another keeps arising in such a way that there is an agglomeration of ideas, images, which need time to be ordered, to have a sense and a meaning.

Once you are aware of all this, you will understand yourself much better, you will understand why many times you have acted impulsively, letting yourself be carried away by the first thing that came to your mind. And it is that in many occasions our actions are automatic, because they are directed by that mechanical movement that takes place in our mind through which you end up being dominated by a series of thoughts that by repeating themselves so much take control of your mind.

We can only stop this mechanism if we are aware that this is how it works. Once we know it, we can establish a certain control over it through a series of instruments and tools that we can use to put a certain balance within us, in that space of consciousness where all those thoughts that often arise without an established order have a place and manifest themselves.

May 26, 2020

Calmness is a great instrument to get to control our mind. It brings us closer to a state in which we are aware of what we think.

To achieve it we must act naturally, without trying to force anything. It only consists of looking for a quiet space, without any noise disturbing us and let our thoughts follow each other, until a moment comes when we realize that the intensity at the mental level decreases. We realize that the mental movement begins to work more slowly and then we can clearly observe what we are thinking at that moment.

Once we are aware of those mental representations, what we should do next is to let them pass, without trying to intervene, without trying to change anything, without acting.

When this situation occurs in which we are calm, in silence, allowing each thought to pass one after the other, we come to have the feeling that we have a certain control over this mechanism, because in that situation we realize that we are not letting ourselves be carried away by the thoughts, our only intention is simply to observe them without intervening, without being influenced too much by them.

This feeling of control over our mental movement can help us to be more and more aware of what is represented in that space. If we manage to reach this point, through calmness, we will have a great tool to analyze ourselves, to observe our thoughts from tranquility, without being conditioned and determined by them. Then we will be able to control, to a certain extent, our mind, which is an automatic mechanism that is very difficult to govern because it works mechanically and most of the time we are not aware of the work it does.

If we get used to observe it calmly, we will discover the characteristics of our thoughts, the contradictions that many times we suffer and that end up wrapping us in a mental confusion that sometimes we do not know how to solve. We will see how our ideas are formed and what it is that alters us. We will discover the mental representations that influence us the most: those that provoke strong emotions in us. We will have the opportunity to observe them and to see their influence on us.

If we manage to analyze ourselves from calm, from tranquility, we can conquer our inner world. We will learn to reflect to detect the causes of what happens to us, so we will find out the origin of our conflicts, the causes of our suffering and what has led us to the situation we are in today.

Each thought can be analyzed, but only if we are in a state of tranquility, of calm. We will be able to take stock of the events that have happened to us, of the reading we have made of them, of the conclusions we have drawn from all that we have experienced in the past. Then we will understand many reactions and ways of acting that we have had in the past.

Calm helps us to understand and know ourselves much better, since it takes us into the depths of our inner world, it makes us see clearly what moves in our mind, what is repeated more often, what determines and conditions us.

Thanks to calmness, a level of communication with yourself is established that cannot be reached in any other way. You get in touch with a source of information that is only there, in a level of consciousness that can only be accessed if you leave aside the noise and everything that distracts you; then you get to know yourself much better and you manage to understand the functioning of that automatic mechanism that determines you without you realizing it: that is your own mind, your human mind.

May 27, 2020

We try to solve our problems through understanding, looking for alternatives within the options that are represented in our mind, which tries to make the necessary movements to obtain as much information as possible in each moment.

Of all the contents that manifest and spread through our consciousness, we must select, most of the time using our common sense, the best alternative. This in principle, because we do not always decide the right thing: we do not opt for the best solution. Sometimes we deviate from common sense and we go down a path that has no way out, we are committed to an idea that leads us nowhere, and so we can be wasting our time for many years, abandoned to a wrong way of thinking.

In these cases, time is the one that puts us in our place, it is the one that takes us out of doubts, through the results that we obtain from all the decisions we have taken previously. It is the best possible judge, the one that makes us go back and rectify when we have made a mistake; it is the one that in the end shows us where the way out is, where the solution is.

Sometimes we are not aware that we are consuming time and that there is no way to recover it. We have already lost the time we have lost, there is no way back. What we can extract from time is its teaching, what we learn through each and every one of the experiences we have the opportunity to experience every day. In this sense, time is valuable, because it is a great learning experience that helps us not to continue making the same mistakes we have been making before; although we do not always rectify, because we can be insisting on the same mistake practically all our lives.

It is true that time gives us the experience and with it the learning we need to solve many difficulties that arise throughout our existence. The time and the experiences we have are the best teachers, because they give us personalized information, adapted to ourselves, because we have been the ones who have lived those experiences and we have been the ones who have made the corresponding reading.

In all this also plays an important role our mind, because it is in charge of ordering all that information that is coming to us from outside, and also of transferring to our memory all those conclusions that we draw from each and every one of the experiences that we are going to live.

An important point in all this process is the way in which we reflect on what happens to us, the conclusions we draw from the situations we live. This influences the representation of the world that in the end we establish in our mind. Our vision of things then influences us when we face the reality of life.

The mental structure that we build up daily with our representation of the world, with our vision of reality, develops in this way. That is why it is important how we interpret things, the reading we make of what happens to us or what we observe happening to others. On this depends our way of acting later, our way of facing difficulties.

May 28, 2020

The mind can suddenly shoot to a set of concrete thoughts, it can suddenly move from one content to another. In these cases it is difficult to exercise control over it, because they are very fast processes that are articulated in a mechanical way. The problem is that this set of thoughts is maintained over time and leads to action, to act in an uncontrolled manner. That is why we often regret our own actions, when we act in an unconscious way, when we follow the dictates of this mechanism and do the first thing that comes to mind.

Sometimes we get lost in this mental movement that flows without rest and that somehow tries to manage us through a current that never stops, that is mechanical and that passes in a very fast way consuming much of our energy. We have to be aware of the need to focus on a certain point, on those thoughts that are beneficial to us, because otherwise this mental movement can take the reins and can lead us to other kinds of elements, of thoughts, which can only lead us to waste time and all the energy that our mind uses in its operation.

The need to pay attention to what is really important to us is a matter of time and energy saving. If we allow our mind to function automatically, at its own free will, it can use up all the energy we have without making us progress. In the end we may feel quite fatigued, but with the feeling that we are still at the same point where we were before. And it is that our mind can only dedicate itself to always going around the same idea, creating vicious circles that capture our attention, causing us to spend our time in unimportant matters, in ideas that are represented there, in our consciousness, but that in reality do not take us anywhere, because they are of no use to us.

It is important that we know at all times where we spend our time and energy. Our mind is like a machine that constantly needs to be fed with thoughts and for that it needs a good amount of energy so that all those contents that arise there can interact and be associated, so that we can draw conclusions and make a series of decisions throughout the day that are necessary for our own survival.

That is why it is necessary that we use it mainly for what can benefit us, since there is the possibility that we can also use it to harm ourselves, especially when we focus or put our attention on a kind of thoughts that are negative, that do not make us move forward, that do not help us to develop, because they have no use, since they only lead us to block and waste time and all that energy that we often need to deal properly with other more important things.

We must bear in mind that, in situations of conflict or of greater difficulty, in our mind there is a greater activity, because we need to use this tool to try to gather as much information as possible to try to give solution to the problem that we have at that moment. Then our mind works tirelessly trying to transport content from our memory to our consciousness so that we can analyze in a more complete way the situation we are in.

When there is a greater accumulation of information and elements, there is a greater expenditure of energy. That is why we feel more tired than usual, both physically and psychologically, when we go through situations of stress and anxiety. In these cases it is recommended that we regain calm, so that our mind returns to tranquility and can function in a normal way, so that it returns to its natural form. We must have enough confidence in ourselves, being aware that, sooner or later, we will find the solution to that conflict that we have at that moment.

May 29, 2020

In reality, it is about learning to overcome the various difficulties that life presents you with. That is why we must take advantage of all those inner capabilities that we all have to somehow get rid of the suffering that we often cause ourselves. In this way we can become a little happier.

This should be our main objective in life. Happiness consists in this: in knowing how to overcome and be above our problems and difficulties. We do not have to look for it elsewhere. It is in ourselves. The only way out of our difficulties is through the knowledge of ourselves, that is the key to everything.

That is why we must learn from our experiences; then we will be much stronger and we will overcome suffering; we will have a much easier life.

It is experience that gives us wisdom, which in reality is what makes us find the truth in the end. The one who tries to seek the truth is an awakened person, he knows how to detect exactly where the adversities are and how to face them.

The awakened person knows how to face problems, but most people are not awakened, they do not have that wisdom. We usually go with the flow without being aware of the power we have inside, which can make us much wiser and help us to be above many inconveniences.

True wisdom is found through the knowledge of ourselves. This is the real power that can help us overcome difficulties, and it is where we can find true knowledge. It is what gives us the ability to overcome every obstacle we encounter along the way, and it is also what gives us faith in ourselves, in that power that we all have within.

Your power is unlimited, but in order to believe and trust in it, we must first know ourselves. Weakness itself comes from not knowing this power we all carry within.

Our true inner power is based on the knowledge we have from all our experiences, and that is what ultimately leads us to success and wisdom. He who is aware of this power knows that he can never fail, even if he loses many battles; it is what gives us faith in ourselves.

Sometimes we think that we cannot manage to live a life different from the one we usually lead, that we are not free, that we are conditioned by many influences, both external and internal. We live in a vicious circle and we hardly feel free to decide our own path. We are tied to the wheel of our own thoughts, of our habits. We carve out, without being very conscious of it, a future from which it is almost impossible to escape.

It is as if we could not aspire to higher things, as if we were living in a situation of slavery, because we are slaves of our desires, of our thoughts and of everything that our mind is proposing to us at every moment.

Some may deny all this, but those who have undergone many changes in their lives become aware that we are very conditioned by a whole series of influences, both external and internal, that are marking our destiny. In such a way that in the end we end up doing things that make our life not worthwhile. It is as if we do not feel free in the depths of ourselves.

There are those who think that it is useless to fight against this mechanism, against our own habits, against this kind of internal conditioning; but in reality, the way we face it all depends on us. We can overcome this conditioning thanks to our own experience; we can observe our inner workings to the point of realizing that there is an inner power hidden in the deepest part of ourselves, which is beyond all that conditions us, beyond all that makes us live a meaningless life.

ABOUT THE AUTHOR

Manuel Triguero has a degree in Psychology from the Pontifical University of Salamanca (Spain). He has provided personalized help, as a counselor, to a large number of people.

In his books he shares his experiences and his own reflections on various topics related to self-knowledge and personal development. They are based on ideas and reflections gained from observation and his own introspection.

The objective is to reveal and make known the power that we all carry within. To access it we must first know ourselves. It is the first step to achieve a "true personal transformation", resolve inner conflicts and thus improve our lives in every way.

They are an invitation to all those interested in this type of content to look inside themselves, awaken their capacity to know themselves and live in the best possible way.

Printed in Great Britain
by Amazon